Voices from Tibet

Voices from Tibet

Selected Essays and Reportage

Tsering Woeser and Wang Lixiong

Edited and translated by Violet S. Law

香港大學出版社
HONG KONG UNIVERSITY PRESS

University of Hawai'i Press
Honolulu

For distribution in Asia, Australia and New Zealand:
Hong Kong University Press
The University of Hong Kong
Pokfulam Road
Hong Kong
www.hkupress.org
ISBN 978-988-8208-11-1 *(Paperback)*

For distribution outside Asia, Australia and New Zealand:
University of Hawai'i Press
2840 Kolowalu Street
Honolulu, Hawai'i 96822 USA
www.uhpress.hawaii.edu
ISBN 978-0-8248-3951-2 *(Paperback)*

Library of Congress Cataloging-in-Publication Data

Voices from Tibet / selected essays and reportage by Tsering Woeser and Wang Lixiong ; edited and translated by Violet S. Law.
    pages cm
    Includes bibliographical references.
    ISBN 978-0-8248-3951-2 (pbk. : alk. paper)
    1. Tibet Autonomous Region (China)—Civilization—20th century. 2. Tibet Autonomous Region (China)—Politics and government—1951- I. Law, Violet S., editor of compilation, translator. II. Weise. Works. Selections. English. III. Wang, Lixiong, Works. Selections. English.
    DS786.V64 2014
    951'.505—dc23
                                                2013034040

10 9 8 7 6 5 4 3 2 1

Printed and bound by Cheer Shine Enteprises Co., Ltd. in Hong Kong, China

Contents

Acknowledgments

Both the authors and I would like to thank Dan Southerland and his staff at Radio Free Asia, where the pieces that make the bulk of this book first aired.

And I am grateful to the authors for their unreserved trust in me. That is not something a translator should take for granted—so surely I do not.

My journey translating *Voices from Tibet* all began with Du Bin, then photographer of *The New York Times*' Beijing bureau haggling with China's equivalent of jitney drivers to ferry me to meet the authors. For all his efforts, I am most thankful.

With his introduction, Robert Barnett put his intimate, incisive knowledge of the authors and their aspirations and conviction for the Tibetans in service of the book, making it so much more than I am able to deliver as a translator. He gave me the much-needed boost to birth this book from a 3,500-word rough-hewn sample.

Peter J. Carroll, Alexander Gardner, Michelle T. King, Julia Lovell, Tsering Shakya, Gray Tuttle, and Jeffrey Wasserstrom—scholars whose interest in their subject is as humanistic as it is academic—have been tremendously encouraging.

I would like to thank all those who took the time and care to comment on my first draft: Donna Scheidt, who, as I did, began the writing life as an undergraduate at the University of Chicago; Christopher Clarke, still the most astute and caring editor I have ever had; and Joseph Boyce, whom I dragged out of retirement from his illustrious journalism career.

I also learned much from the eagle-eyed editing of maestro transla-
tors Martin Merz and Jane Weizhen Pan. Hats off to Martin Alexander
and Kathleen Hwang of *Asia Literary Review* for publishing an excerpt.

I am much obliged to Dan Friedman and Freda Wan for their gracious
hospitality in Beijing, where I worked with the authors to bring this book
to fruition.

As always and ever, I am indebted to my ever-loving and understanding aunt Shiu Min, whose serene and sun-filled home in Vancouver,
Canada, surpasses any writer's retreat on earth. It was there I sat down
and started to translate. For her patience and prescience, as well as her
abiding interest in my words and work, I will make every endeavor to be
a much better writer than I have ever dreamed of being.

Last but surely not least, I am grateful to Michael Duckworth, now
publisher of University of Hawai'i Press and formerly of Hong Kong
University Press, for believing in this book from the very beginning.

V. S. L.

Introduction

Robert Barnett

> I know if I don't speak now,
> I'll be silent forever
>> —Tsering Woeser, "December" (1995)[1]

Viewed from space, Tibet is one of those distinct zones on the globe that can immediately be recognized—a vast, landlocked plateau ringed by the highest mountains in the world, threaded with glaciers and riven by the upper valleys of some of the world's mightiest rivers, among them the Indus, the Brahmaputra, the Irrawaddy, the Salween, the Mekong, the Yangtze, and the Yellow River. Three and a half times the size of Texas, as large as western Europe minus Scandinavia, it has a population of around 6 million Tibetans, with an average density of little more than six people per square mile, plus an unknown number of non-Tibetan migrants, perhaps around 1–2 million in total. Much of the plateau consists of uninhabited tundra to the northwest and thinly vegetated grasslands to the east, most of it at some 12,000 feet or more above sea level, with yak- and sheep-herders on the grasslands and barley farmers in the lower valleys, clustered around what were once small towns and their protective forts, now being speedily converted into modern cities.

Fourteen hundred years ago, when horsemanship was the most important element of war, Tibetans were a major force in eastern Eurasia, with an empire that included much of what is now western China and

---

1. Tsering Woeser, *Tibet's True Heart*, tr. A. E. Clark (Dobbs Ferry, NY: Ragged Banner Press, 2008), 12.

parts of central and southern Asia too. By the thirteenth century they had long been eclipsed as a military power by their nomadic neighbors to the northeast, the Mongols, and Tibet became politically less prominent, a vast but little-noticed nation lying between the modern giants of east and southern Asia—China, the British Empire and, later, India. The Manchus, before they came to power in Beijing in 1644 as Qing emperors, showed a consistent and intense interest in Tibet. From the 1720s onwards, they stationed commissioners in Lhasa, the Tibetan capital, together with a contingent of some 200–300 soldiers, and treated the area as, in some undefined way, a part of their empire.

But during the eighteenth and nineteenth centuries, Tibetans were left to run their country largely by themselves. The work of government, at least in central Tibet, lay almost entirely in the hands of some 250 aristocratic families who, together with the leading monasteries, owned much of the rural land and supplied the officials who ran the government under the leadership of the Dalai Lama. This system made agreement on reform almost impossible, leaving the country increasingly far behind the rest of Asia in terms of technology, ideas, defense, industry and infrastructure. Some progress was made whenever an exceptionally able Dalai Lama remained in power for more than a few years, but this only happened twice before 1950, once with the Fifth Dalai Lama in the seventeenth century (r. 1642–1682) and again with the thirteenth of that line in the early twentieth century (r. 1895–1933). The other Dalai Lamas made little impact or died at about the time they were expected to take over power, presumably at the hands of the regents who were meant to cede their thrones to them.

The situation changed in 1903, when Tibet was invaded by a British army based in India. The British forced the Lhasa government to sign a humiliating surrender, leaving Beijing with little choice but to respond decisively to this foreign intrusion into its sphere of influence: it decided to end all ambiguity about Tibet's status by turning the area into an integral part of China. Its first attempt to do so was in 1910, when it sent an army to take over Lhasa, aiming to set up a provincial government. Within a year, the Xinhai Revolution in Beijing deposed the

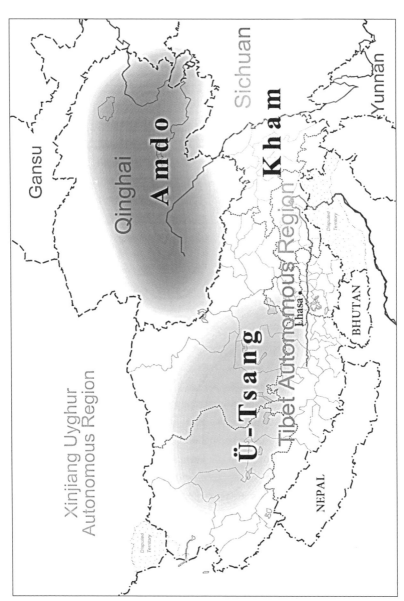

Map 1   The Tibetan Regions (based on: http://commons.wikimedia.org/wiki/File:Tibet_provinces.png)

Manchu emperors for good, leaving their soldiers in Lhasa unpaid and unsupplied, enabling the Tibetan army to defeat them. For the next three decades, while China was wracked by invasion and civil war, Tibet was effectively independent.

Tibet's government, however, failed to get any foreign countries to recognize its claims to independence, and, when the Chinese Communist Party finally came to power in Beijing in 1949, there was little the Tibetan government could do to avoid invasion. Their pleas to the United Nations and to the British were unsuccessful, and in October 1950 their army was easily outnumbered and outgunned by the troops of the People's Liberation Army. Seven months later, the Tibetan government signed an agreement in Beijing that for the first time in history acknowledged in writing that Tibet was "within the boundaries of China" and that "the Tibetan people shall return to the big family of the motherland." Since that moment, Tibet has been officially a part of China, an administrative region run by a Communist government, and firmly situated within the current Chinese state.

* * *

This was the Tibet into which, fifteen years after the signing of that agreement, the poet, essayist and campaigner Tsering Woeser was born. The daughter of a senior officer in the People's Liberation Army, Woeser was born in Lhasa in 1966, capital of the area that had been renamed just one year earlier the Tibet Autonomous Region (TAR). This term has been used since then for the only area recognized by the Chinese government as Tibet—the central and western parts of the Tibetan plateau, which had been the areas ruled directly by the previous Dalai Lama in the 1940s. But from the age of four Woeser was brought up in Tawu, and later in Dartsendo (Kangding in Chinese), Tibetan towns in western Sichuan, not far from her father's hometown of Derge, just to the east of the current border of the TAR. The new Tibetan elite among whom Woeser was raised were part of a Chinese cultural world, an enclave of modernity and progress populated by officers, officials and their families in what must have seemed to most of them a distant, backward and remote locality. At that time, there were no classes in Tibetan at the schools that she attended, and for pupils such as her, Tibetan became the language of conversation, while Chinese was used for reading and writing.

All monasteries in Tibet had been closed some five or ten years before Woeser was born, and in many cases their contents had been ransacked and destroyed. All property had been seized from those deemed to be class enemies and redistributed to the peasants, who were reorganized into communes. This had led to armed resistance by Tibetans in the provinces of Sichuan and Qinghai, as well as other areas, culminating in a major uprising in Lhasa in March 1959, the failure of which had led the Dalai Lama and some 80,000 other Tibetans to flee to exile in India. A campaign of retribution had followed throughout Tibet, with terrible consequences for all those suspected of any involvement in resistance. It was one of innumerable campaigns that were to follow in the two decades after 1959, both in Tibet as in China, as the new government sought to reshape society, redistribute land, boost production, and eradicate class difference.

In the year that Woeser was born, the Cultural Revolution was launched throughout China, with aims even more far-reaching than those of the previous decade and a half: to destroy traditional thought, to eradicate old customs, and to wipe out old or bourgeois thinking. Most of these efforts ended up in violence, with monks and nuns forced to disrobe, while former landlords, lamas and teachers were regularly paraded in the streets, where they were harangued, pilloried, or struggled against in public by youths just ten or fifteen years older than Woeser. Children of her age would probably have known little then of these events, or of the tens of thousands of Tibetans and others killed or maimed in waves of fighting, uprisings, elimination campaigns, lynchings, policy-driven famines and imprisonment that had taken place across the Tibetan plateau in response to the land reforms and monastery destruction after 1955, or of similar events in China as a whole. Most younger people in Tibetan areas still know little of these events, and older ones have been encouraged to forget them.

As a child, Woeser would have known that she was Tibetan, but everything around her would have emphasized her identity as a citizen of a new and thrusting Chinese state, one which at that time celebrated socialism above all other values, fostering radical egalitarianism together with a sometimes violent distrust of religion, tradition, past culture, the bourgeoisie and foreign imperialists. Apart from proletarian folk dance and songs, almost everything Tibetan would probably have been regarded as opaque and backward, if sometimes quaint, while progress and modernity would have been associated with Chinese culture and society. This was state ideology for nearly three decades from the early 1950s, and it is unlikely that many would have questioned it during that time.

* * *

Wang Lixiong also grew up in the new, socialist, and modernizing China. But his childhood, spent in Changchun, a city 2000 miles to the north-east of Lhasa, was very different from that of Woeser, his future wife. Founded as a fur-trading outpost in the sixteenth century, Changchun was situated within Manchuria, an area that, like Tibet, lay on the edges of the former Qing empire, part of an outer domain that had been the homeland of a nomadic, Inner Asian people wholly different from the majority Chinese. But by the early twentieth century, Manchuria had long lost any traces of ethnic difference: it had been repopulated by ethnic Chinese, now known as Han; the trading post had become a major city; the original language of the region had all but died out; and Manchu culture and nomadic lifestyle had disappeared. Eleven thousand feet lower in altitude than Lhasa, far colder in the winters, and with a population some forty times that of the Tibetan capital, Changchun had become by the 1950s a major industrial city and the center of the auto-motive industry in the newly founded People's Republic.

In 1953, when Wang was born, the city had just survived a half-century of war, invasion, occupation, plague and siege. Wang's mother was a writer at the famous Changchun Film Studio, no doubt the source of her son's lifelong interest in writing as a profession. His father, Wang

Shaolin, held a leading position in one of the city's car factories, where his subordinates are said to have included the future Chinese president, Jiang Zemin, a connection that may explain why the younger Wang and his wife have so far been able to escape long-term detention despite their dissident writings and research.

Just as Wang was reaching his formative years, the Cultural Revolution brought tragedy to the family: in 1968 his father, like so many of the intellectuals, leaders, teachers and others who were persecuted at that time, committed suicide whilst in custody. In 1969, Wang was sent to work in the countryside, but after four years he was rehabilitated, deemed to be a model worker, and permitted to attend the Jilin University of Technology as a *gongnongbing daxuesheng*—a worker-peasant-soldier university student.

Wang was in his final year at university when Mao's death in 1976 brought an end to the radical era and the mass violence that it had entailed. The new and more pragmatic leadership under Deng Xiaoping reclassified the Cultural Revolution as "ten years of disaster," ended the practice of basing all policy on the fight against class enemies, and shifted China to a policy known as "reform and opening up," which allowed private wealth, university education, and international exchanges. The mood of the country became one of exhilaration, optimism and relative relaxation.

While still in the countryside Wang had already started writing poetry, and as a student in 1975 he had compiled notes on an alternative political system which he called "stage democracy," the concept of facilitating gradual political transition by establishing democratic procedures from the village level upwards. In 1978, while working as a car-factory mechanic, he published his first short story in the prominent dissident magazine, *Jintian* (Today). Two years later, as a tide of post-revolutionary thought and art swept across China, he left the car factory determined to become a writer. His first works were film scripts, but in 1983 he published a novella, *Yongdongji huanzhe* (Victim of a Perpetual Motion Machine). Like all his later fiction, it was an allegorical, futuristic commentary on contemporary Chinese politics, describing a farmer's attempts to invent an impossible machine in order to lift his family out of poverty.

In the mid-1980s, new and dynamic approaches to art and literature appeared, such as Scar Literature, Root-seeking, and Misty Poetry. These focused on individual experience, suffering, identity, and heritage, and treated cultural difference and ethnic distinctiveness as vibrant parts of Chinese culture and as sources of self-knowledge for aspiring Chinese artists. In this climate, Wang joined the many Chinese artists, writers and intellectuals who traveled to the Tibetan areas in the search for pre-modern sensations and experiences that could no longer be found in the towns and villages of modern China.

Wang's first journey to these areas was in 1984. It was literally a search for the source: he traveled to the headwaters of the Yellow River, and then floated 800 miles downstream alone on a raft made from the inner tubes of truck tires. This became the subject of a book, *Piaoliu* (Drifting), in 1988. Unlike many of his fellow intellectuals, he seems to have viewed the experience as a test of personal endurance and capacity rather than as an enrichment of personal experience or an enhancement of artistic status. Furthermore, he used his journey to call Chinese people to devote serious attention to issues of environmental preservation, becoming one of the first people in China to raise this issue. It was this journey along the Yellow River that first brought him into close contact both with civic issues and with Tibetans and other peoples beyond the Chinese heartlands.

* * *

Woeser was ten years old when Mao died and his ultra-leftist policies were finally reversed. But her memory of these experiences would have been far less vivid than Wang's, and as she grew up, open discussion of the Cultural Revolution was increasingly discouraged within China and barely tolerated at all within Tibet. It would be some twenty years before she would come to learn about the details of that history. As a teenager, her main sources of influence and inspiration, evident in all her later writing, would have been the new approaches to art and subjectivity that were flourishing in the mid-1980s, when she entered a university in Chengdu, the capital of Sichuan, to study Chinese literature. For her, the Tibetan plateau was a home, rather than an exotic locale or a proving ground, and after graduating in 1988, it became her workplace too: she went to work as a reporter for the official Party paper in Dartsendo, the capital of Kardze (Ganzi in Chinese), one of the two Tibetan prefectures within Sichuan, where she had been brought up. Two years later, she was posted to the offices of the Tibetan Branch of the Chinese Writers' Association, a government body in Lhasa, the city of her birth. There she was appointed to work as an editor of the association's journal, *Xizang wenxue* (Tibet Literature).

By the time she took up her position with the government in Lhasa, major change was underway in both Tibet and China. The return to the household economy in the previous decade had led to a sharp rise in incomes and prosperity across China, and in Tibet a vast program of government investment and subsidy was leading to radical changes in the urban landscape too. But politically the situation had become much tighter. Across China, large numbers of protesters had died or been imprisoned after the protests of June 1989, when students and workers across the country had called for increased democracy and an end to corruption among officials. Throughout the country, drives to enforce political re-education, Marxist theory, and Party loyalty were being carried out in schools, universities, offices and villages to deter any further challenges to the system. In Lhasa, living conditions were more restrictive than those in China generally or in the eastern Tibetan areas where Woeser had been brought up. The city of Lhasa and the surrounding area had been under martial law since March 1989, following a series of protests calling for Tibetan independence that had begun in September 1987. These had led to numerous arrests, long prison sentences, and the deaths of 100 or so Tibetans shot by paramilitary troops or by the police during demonstrations. In 1992, conditions for Tibetans, Uighurs, Mongols and other non-Chinese nationalities in China became even more restrictive following the fall of the Soviet Union, which was attributed by Chinese analysts in part to overly lax policies towards minority nationalities.

For Tibetans like Woeser, there was probably little if any contact with those Tibetans who were involved in dissent, most of whom were monks and nuns or market-traders and shop-workers. At that time, few Tibetan students, intellectuals, artists, or officials admitted any connection to those caught up in the unrest in Lhasa, and nobody with a position in the bureaucracy, and few others of any kind, dared to speak about political issues, even to their friends or family members, except when required to express loyalty to the Party and the state. In any case, many Tibetans at that time considered protest and dissent pointless or damaging. After all, economic conditions were rapidly improving, at least in towns, and, although political conditions had become more restrictive than during the early 1980s, the situation was still far more congenial and relaxed than it had been during the Cultural Revolution.

Among the Tibetans whom Woeser met and worked with in Lhasa at that time, the focus was probably on the effort to create a new Tibetan culture without touching on political affairs. When the first literary journal was started in Tibet in 1977, the editors had found few modern Tibetan writers; its first issues had consisted of writings by Chinese stationed in Tibet, and Tibetan-language stories had been translations from a handful of Tibetans writing in Chinese. Even when Tibetan writers emerged who could write in their own language, most of their published work in the early 1980s had followed statist lines, being mainly descriptions of the former backward Tibetan society from which the CCP had liberated them. From the mid-1980s onwards a growing number of educated Tibetans tried to fill that gap by becoming writers, poets or artists. Celebrating China's magnanimity in bringing modernity to its minorities was not a theme of importance to this generation. For them, a notion that was more important was *la rgya*, the Tibetan word for loyalty, meaning in this context pride in one's nationality and in being a Tibetan, and one way of expressing *la rgya* was to write short stories or poems that featured Tibetan culture and heritage, whether in Tibetan or Chinese.

Woeser was already writing poetry before she returned to Lhasa. As a student in Chengdu and during her time as a reporter in Dartsendo she had written poems that already bore what would become the trademark features of her style: impressionistic, allusive, and poignant, with cryptic imagery. They recalled the work of Misty poets like Yang Lian, who had been inspired by his time in Lhasa in the early 1980s, and the revered Tibetan writer from Amdo, Yidam Tsering, some thirty years older than Woeser, who like her was able to write only in Chinese. Her early works, though difficult to interpret, have few explicit references to Tibetan culture; they deal with issues of personal emotion and identity. The first one that she recalls, written when she was eighteen, shows already sophistication in the leanness of its style and the restrained deployment of metaphor, combined with a fierce sense of national identity:

> Never again let
> muddy water of disdain
> flow from your young eyes
> The print that exudes
> the scent of butter *tsampa*
> is engraved on my heart[2]

After graduating from university, however, Woeser became more involved in aestheticism and the life of the poet, and less certain of the importance of collective identity. In "Positionings," written in 1988, she questions her Tibetanness, offering a wry comment on the apparent benefits of forgetting one's origins: "It's often better not to think too much . . . It's hard to forget home, and that's what'll get you into trouble."[3]

Her return to Lhasa brought a partial change, an engagement with Tibetan landscape, history and people. These became the primary elements of her writing. We catch glimpses of encounters with Tibetans in the countryside, conversations with lamas, visits to temples and mountains, and references to earlier Tibetan literature. Deeply affected by the sudden death of her father in December 1991, and by her realization that he may secretly have retained a deep but hidden reverence for

---

2.   Woeser, "Print—For Certain Prejudices," tr. Fiona Sze-Lorrain, cited in Dechen Pemba and Woeser, "An Eye from History and Reality—Woeser and the Story of Tibet," *Cerise Press* 3(9), Spring 2012.

3.   Woeser, *Tibet's True Heart*, 79.

Buddhism, Tibetan religion too emerges as an increasingly important resource in her work.

By 1995, her poems began to include references not just to questions of belief and culture, but to political concerns as well. The specifics of those issues were still heavily veiled, but the concern was clear. The poem "December," written in 1995, was a turning-point in her journey from the aesthetic to the political. It begins with a direct critique of the typical rhetoric used by officials to describe the situation in Tibet:

> "Hear Ye!" The big lie shall blot the sky,
> Two sparrows in the woods shall fall.
> "Tibet", he says, "Tibet is fine and flourishing."[4]

Nothing else in the poem explains what has prompted Woeser's accusation, nor who is being accused, and one can only know from context who the sparrows are. Their identity is hinted at in the title: in December 1995, the Chinese authorities staged a highly publicized ceremony in Lhasa at which they selected through a lottery, later shown to have been rigged, a five-year-old boy of their choosing to be the Eleventh Panchen Lama, one of the highest-ranking dignitaries in the Tibetan religious system. Another Tibetan child had been detained seven months earlier by Beijing (his whereabouts remain unknown), because he had been recognized by the exile Dalai Lama as the reincarnation of the Panchen Lama. The "two sparrows" are probably these two boys, both victims in different ways of the "big lie" of the December lottery.

There were other developments which might have led Woeser to shift from concern about the condition of Tibetan culture and identity to anger about the treatment of that culture by officials in Lhasa and Beijing. In July 1994, the Chinese authorities had made an unexpected change in policy: they launched a denunciation drive against the Dalai Lama, which continues to this day. Previously, he had been often condemned by China for his political opinions, blamed for the occasional protests that had occurred in Lhasa after 1987, and excoriated for raising the Tibet issue in his frequent, high-profile visits to the West. But the new

---

4.   Woeser, "December," in *Tibet's True Heart*, 12.

campaign attacked him ad hominem, denouncing him as an individual and as a religious leader. Within a year, orders were issued banning public display of his photograph within Tibet, prayers or ceremonies addressed to him were outlawed, and eventually people's homes were searched in some areas to see if they had such photographs. A personal denunciation drive of this kind was unprecedented in the post-Mao era, even after the Tiananmen Square protests of 1989, let alone one that vilified a major religious leader. It had always been understood that official claims by the Chinese state to respect religious belief of any kind were heavily circumscribed; that is the case in all states to some extent, and especially so in socialist ones. But to attack Tibetans' most highly regarded religious teacher in personal terms, and to organize saturation coverage of such attacks in the media, must have seemed disturbing and provocative to Tibetans, including some of those who until that time had stood on the sidelines of political debate. In Lhasa, the policy was taken much further: all Tibetan government employees, their family members, and all Tibetan students were told that they were no longer allowed to have Buddhist shrines or objects in their homes or in their dormitories. They were also banned from visiting temples or monasteries and from taking part in religious activities. This policy, which was never written down or publicized, would have applied to Woeser and to other Tibetan intellectuals who had government positions.

Few if any writers in Tibet at this time revealed their opinion of this sharp downturn in China's approach to Tibetan culture and religion. But Woeser's poems in the late 1990s increasingly hint, through indirect language and veiled images, at the strains of living in Tibet under those conditions. When the first volume of her poetry was published in 1999, *Xizang zai shang* (Tibet Above), it was well received in China and she was widely noted as an interesting new literary voice, a Tibetan who could write exceptionally well in Chinese and who used a modern, rich, and imagistic idiom. Cultural pride by members of minorities was valued then in China, seen as adding exoticness to the treasure-house of Chinese literature and culture; it was not perceived as political. Reading back, one can see that her cultural pride had taken more specific form and that increasingly she was thinking about the causes of cultural loss, rather than just the loss itself. But if references to political issues had been apparent to the publishers or Chinese readers, it is unlikely that the 1999 volume would have been published within China or admired within literary circles there.

* * *

During his first fifteen years as a writer, Wang approached the questions of democracy and politics primarily through fiction. He became known to the Chinese public for the novel *Huanghuo* (Yellow Peril, 1991), an apocalyptic account of an imaginary future in which a chance environmental disaster leads to the downfall of the Chinese state. The title refers not to western fears of Chinese domination, but to the Yellow River, which in the story bursts its banks during a freak storm, flooding major cities and triggering a chain of catastrophic events that include political turmoil, the emergence of extremist militant environmentalist gangs ("Green Guards"), secessionist movements in outlying areas of the country, and civil war between the northern and southern parts of China. As the fighting escalates, the one-party system in China finally unravels, triggering worldwide war as the US and Russia invade other countries in order to obtain provisions for their populations. The book, with its implied critique of the CCP, could not have been published within China and so appeared in Hong Kong with the author identified only by the pseudonym Bao Mi (Keep secret).[5]

Huanghuo was ranked among the 100 most influential Chinese novels in the twentieth century by a Hong Kong magazine and enjoyed some success among the reading public in China. It was, like his other novels, a work of "political prophecy fiction" designed to propose serious political questions to his readers rather than to provide entertainment or financial success. From 1991, he returned to theoretical writing, producing a book-length study of his early ideas about gradualist democratization;

---

5.   *Huanghuo* has been translated into English as *China Tidal Wave: A Novel*,
      tr. Anton Platero (Folkestone: Global Oriental, 2008).

a second volume on the same theme followed six years later.[6] But as a political thinker and activist, he was better known for his pioneering work on environmental issues. In 1994, ten years after he had first drawn attention to environmental issues in China by his solo journey down the Yellow River, he played an important role in the development of civil society in China: he became one of the co-founders of China's first officially acknowledged NGO, the environmental campaign group, Friends of Nature (*Ziran zhi you*).

By that time he had already begun to turn his attention to more sensitive issues, ones that few independent Chinese writers had touched. After his first river journey, he had returned a dozen or more times to the Tibetan areas within China, and had lived in the region for more than two years. Drawing on extensive reading, interviews and observation in those years, Wang published a book in 1998 about the Tibetan-China dispute called *Tianzang: Xizang de mingyun* (Sky Burial: The Destiny of Tibet). It was hailed within China for its depth of detail and historical knowledge and was widely seen as the first independent study of the controversy by a Chinese writer. Other independent Chinese artists and intellectuals had written about Tibet, but mainly to describe its culture, ethos or landscape rather than to research its history or politics. "For the most part," as the intellectual historian Wang Chaohua wrote from exile in 2003, "Chinese intellectuals have so far locked out the nationalities question from their concerns, as if it had no bearing on China's future."[7] *Tianzang* was enthusiastically received by Chinese intellectuals, particularly those in the diaspora, who saw in his work a way of responding to western criticisms of China's Tibet policies without damaging China's claims or national pride.

---

6.   Wang Lixiong, *Rongjie quanli: zhuceng di xuanzhi* [Dissolving power: A successive multi-level electoral system] (Mississauga, Ontario: Mirror Books, 1998), and *Dijin minzhu—Zhongguo de di san tiao daolu* [Incremental democracy: China's third road] (Hong Kong: Social Science Publishing House, 2004).

7.   Wang Chaohua (ed.), "Introduction," in *One China, Many Paths* (London: Verso, 2003), 43. See also Steven L. Venturino, "Inquiring after Theory in China," *boundary* 2, 2006, 33(2): 91–113.

But the Tibetan intelligentsia inside China was more suspicious about *Tianzang*. Communicating privately rather than in print, they wrote of a residual essentialism or condescension that they detected in Wang's writing, reminiscent of an earlier tradition in CCP writing of describing non-Chinese peoples within China as "younger brother nationalities." Such criticisms invoked larger questions of cultural politics. The leading Western-trained exile Tibetan historian, Tsering Shakya, in a critique of Wang's early writing on the issue, accused him of "crude environmental determinism," and described his interpretation at that time of Tibetan political views as an example of "the colonial attitudes of the Chinese intelligentsia."[8]

That was soon to change: Wang had not only an unrivalled capacity for research, but an unusual openness to debate and criticism. His thinking constantly evolved. His subsequent writing on Tibet and other issues adapted to accommodate criticisms from others, demonstrating a respect for the views of the subaltern in any situation as well as a commitment to rational argument and extensive research. These led to him being widely respected in China even among those who disagreed strongly with his views. He became less an analyst looking from the outside at another people and more an individual attempting to understand and articulate that people's view of their history and predicament. As he put it later, what became important to him was not collecting facts or marshaling expertise, but to document "the mournings and hopes of an ancient people [to] survive."[9]

In 2001 Wang wrote a uniquely critical study of the situation in Xinjiang, another deeply troubled area of China,[10] which he published

8. Tsering W. Shakya, "Blood in the Snows: Reply to Wang Lixiong," *New Left Review* 15 (May–June 2002): 39–60; see http://newleftreview.org/II/15/tsering-shakya-blood-in-the-snows. All internet references in this chapter were accessible as of July 8, 2013. For a book-length version of the debate between the two writers, see Wang Lixiong and Tsering Shakya, *The Struggle for Tibet* (London: Verso, 2009).

9. Cited in Pemba and Woeser, "An Eye from History and Reality."

10. Wang Lixiong, *Wo de Xiyu, ni de Dongtu* [My West China, your East Turkestan] (Taipei: Dakuai wenhua [Locus Publishing], 2007).

in Taiwan. That same year, he resigned from the Chinese Writers' Association, which he had joined in 1988, issuing a public statement in which he denounced any form of collaboration with the government:

> It is no longer acquiescence which is demanded, but the annihilation of the whole personality, of all conscience and of all individual pride, in order to make crouching dogs of us. To continue to belong to this organization is not an honor, it is on the contrary the shame of any writer worthy of the name.[11]

Shortly afterwards, the environmental group that he had helped to found, Friends of Nature, was ordered by the government to expel him from the organization, reportedly because of his work on Tibet and Xinjiang. Unlike many of his fellow writers, since then he has had no linkage to any government entity or official publication, and no position in any institution.

* * *

By the end of the millennium, the signs of Woeser's concerns had become more evident. One poem, written in 2000, took an image from a famously ambiguous song released five years earlier by the leading Tibetan singer Yadong ("Xiangwang shenying," or "Yearning for the sacred eagle"), and applied it in less oblique terms to an exiled hero, without mention of his name:

> The eagle of my spirit
> Was wounded by a demon,
> Shocked into flight.
> It makes me weep to think of it.[12]

---

11. Cited in Rémi Quesnel, "Wang Lixiong, an Atypical Intellectual," *China Perspectives*, No. 50 (2003), para 37. Posted online in English on 19 April 2007 at http://chinaperspectives.revues.org/document776.html. Wang's original letter is available in Chinese as "Tuichu Zhongguo Zuojiaxiehui de gongkaixin" [Open letter of withdrawal from the Chinese Writers' Association], May 2, 2001, http://wlx.sowiki.net//?action=show&id=251.

12. Woeser, "Coming Home," in *Tibet's True Heart*, 78.

Tibetan pop singers had increasingly begun to test the boundaries of censorship during the 1990s by inserting veiled references to the Dalai Lama in their songs, but this was one of the earliest pieces of modern Tibetan literature to do that within Tibet. It was also one of the first signs of Woeser's growing admiration for the Tibetan leader.

In 2003, Woeser moved from poetry to prose, releasing a collection of essays on her experiences in Tibet called *Xizang biji* (Notes on Tibet, 2003). In prose, her style changed from reliance on allusive imagery to reportage that more or less rendered her moral concerns explicit. The style and format of these pieces were literary and anecdotal, and they made few explicitly political remarks. Instead, they were stories about individual Tibetans and their feelings in everyday situations. But they included references to sensitive issues and ideas, such as the stories that Tibetans are forced by the Chinese government to tell foreigners, the private contempt felt by many Tibetans towards the government, the lack of education and civility among government officials in Tibet, and the sympathy felt by the author for Tibetan exiles and their views.

The book was published in an area of eastern China where these impressionistic tales probably appeared relatively personal and uncontentious, since expression was and is so much freer in ethnic Chinese areas of China than it is in Tibet; in addition, apparently the publisher did not know who the Dalai Lama was. But when the essays came to the attention of officials in Lhasa, the book was banned. Woeser was dismissed from her position there for "stepping into the wrong political domain," "praising the Dalai Lama and the Karmapa, encouraging belief in religion," and "having the wrong political stance." This was a dangerous situation for a Tibetan, and a person of lesser stature facing such accusations would have been at serious risk from the TAR authorities. Woeser moved immediately to Beijing, where the TAR officials had less influence, and began a new career as a solitary, unpaid, unofficial spokeswoman for Tibetan dissidents within China, first as an essayist on Tibetan issues, then as a compiler of information about events in Tibetan areas, and then as a commentator on the Internet and in the foreign media. She became the first and only Tibetan living in China to survive as a public critic of Chinese policy without being arrested.

Woeser has succeeded thus far, but operates under stringent limitations. Her work cannot be published within China, appearing instead in Taiwan or in other foreign countries. Her blog postings are hosted on a foreign website to which there is no legal access from within China. She has been repeatedly refused a passport (despite once unsuccessfully taking the government to court over this issue) and lives under close surveillance with Wang in Beijing, with periods when security officials do not allow them to leave the apartment. She is thus, at the time of writing, the only Tibetan within China who is able to continue openly defying censorship and speaking directly to foreigners about political events in Tibet. She is a unique historical aberration in the sixty years since China took over Tibet, a critical voice that has continued to speak out from within the country in a world and at a time where all others have been silenced.

Why has Woeser been the only Tibetan to succeed in such a role? Her and Wang's family connections may have helped, as has her international stature. But the principal factors seem to have been boldness and ingenuity. By moving to Beijing, she in effect embarrassed officials into handling her case in the way they deal with ethnic Chinese intellectuals, rather than their Tibetan counterparts. Tibetan political activists within Tibet tend to express their most outspoken views in leaflets or books, which invariably leads to arrest, but by switching from print to social media, like most ethnic Chinese dissidents, Woeser gamed the system, and gained more time. In addition, she writes about politics in a way that is strong, assertive and emotionally informed, but generally not polemical. She tends to focus on particular issues and events and to attack bad policies relating to these, rooting her critiques in details rather than generalities. Her language appeals to sentiment, but the arguments are generally well constructed and rational, only occasionally drawing on broad concepts such as independence, occupation, or oppression. In addition, many of the issues that she raises are about China's cultural policies in Tibet, rather than its historic claim to ownership of Tibet. But the key reason may be simply that she confused officials by doing something no other Tibetan had tried before.

* * *

Wang's ideas and approach show a marked change at around the time he met Woeser. After publishing *Tianzang*, he had produced an important essay on the Tibetan issue, his 1999 commentary, "The PRC's 21st Century Underbelly."[13] This was a discussion of the urgent need for China to solve the problem of Tibet and thus an argument appealing primarily to the interests of the state. He had always been aware of the importance of cultural questions when considering China and its history, and had written about this in a 1995 essay on the crisis of belief in China, the so-called "spiritual vacuum":

> I think the most realistic prospect and the most serious crisis [facing the] future China are less [related] to its politics and economy than to the disintegration of the cultural structure. Mere politics and economy are at shallow layers of the society and their crisis, if any, is not difficult to pass, but the spiritual chaos caused by the disintegration of the cultural structure can bring fundamental destruction upon the society. . . . Political structure and economic structure can be readjusted and even rebuilt within a few years or a few decades, but the formation of a cultural structure must take several centuries or even a thousand years . . .
>
> Of course, the disintegration of the cultural structure will not lead immediately to the disintegration of the society. Lives of several generations are just a blink in the long river of history and one perhaps may not feel doomed in his everyday life. Put a frog into the boiling water and it will at once jump out, but heat the cold water up slowly and the frog will drift in the water, fall to sleep comfortably and finally die unawares.[14]

---

13. Wang Lixiong, "Xizang: Ershiyi shiji Zhongguo de ruanle" [The PRC's 21st century underbelly], *Beijing zhanlüe yu guanli*, January 2, 1999, p. 21, and also *Ta Kung Pao*, Hong Kong, March 31, 1999, p. C8. Available in translation by the BBC Survey of World Broadcasts at www.columbia.edu/itc/ealac/barnett/pdfs/link14-wang-lixiong.pdf.

14. Wang Lixiong, "Disintegration and Doom of Chinese Cultural Structure," 2010 (1995), available in translation at http://sotopia.net/democracy/archives/113 or http://wlx.sowiki.net/?action=show&id=10.

In the 1990s, however, he had not applied this perspective when writing about minorities.[15] But during a month in prison in Xinjiang in 1999, after being detained for copying an internal document, he was deeply affected by conversations with his Uighur cellmate. And his encounter with Woeser at this time had a formative effect on his understanding: as he put it later, over the years she "introduced him to Tibet's emotional world, inaccessible through research alone."[16] His approach to Tibetan and other issues shifted from economistic or structuralist interpretations, which tend to carry with them the assumption that minorities are relatively backward, to framings based in complex questions of culture and understanding. At the same time, he widened his interactions with Tibetans from different backgrounds, traveling in 2000 to the US to meet with Tibetan exiles, and in particular with Chinese-educated Tibetans living abroad. His conversations with them led to meetings in the US with the Dalai Lama's chief negotiator, and then with the Dalai Lama himself the following spring.

He discussed these encounters at length in a series of extended essays and a book,[17] in which he sought to explain to fellow Chinese why he considered a negotiated settlement with the Dalai Lama to be the key to resolving the Tibetan issue. Increasingly, he engaged his readers not just through logic and rational argument, but through stories and anecdotes about human encounters, using his skills as a narrative writer to produce pieces rich in human interest, color and description.

15. Wang's first publication in a major English-language journal, "Reflections on Tibet" (*New Left Review* 14 (March–April 2002): 79–111), critiqued by Tsering Shakya, was a reprint of an article written in the 1990s and so reflected an earlier stage of his thinking on Tibetan issues.

16. Wang and Shakya, *The Struggle for Tibet*, 277.

17. Wang Lixiong, "Dalai Lama Is the Key to the 'Tibetan Question,'" July 2000, published in translation in C. X. George Wei and Xiaoyuan Liu (eds.), *Exploring Nationalism of China: Themes and Conflicts* (Westport, CT: Greenwood Press, 2002), 151–72, see http://wlx.sowiki.net/?action= show&id=1. See also "My Four Meetings with Dalai Lama," 2001, available in translation at http://sotopia.net/democracy/archives/91 and *Yu Dalai Lama duihua* [Dialogue with the Dalai Lama] (Skokie, IL: Renjian Publishing, 2002).

Wang also met at this time with Tibetans within China, who would have an important impact on his work. Traveling in 2001 in a Tibetan area of Sichuan not far south of Woeser's birthplace, he met with the lama Tenzin Delek, little known outside his area and with no record of political activity. But a year later the lama was accused by the Sichuan authorities citing evidence that seemed doubtful. Wang became not just a commentator but a campaigner and legal advocate for the lama. He wrote detailed essays recalling his conversations with the lama and questioned the prosecution's case against him,[18] and later organized a defense team, coordinated a petition by twenty-four Chinese intellectuals calling for a fair and open trial, and petitioned China's Supreme Court on his behalf.[19] The campaign failed—Tenzin Delek received a suspended death sentence, later reduced to a life sentence—but it was one of the first times that Chinese intellectuals and lawyers had supported a Tibetan case, and it led to important writing by Wang about the essential social role of lamas as moral exemplars in contemporary Tibetan society.[20]

Increasingly, Wang took to writing in detail about specific events and incidents in Tibetan life, bringing to light the workings of the state at the granular level in his effort to describe the nature of Chinese rule as experienced by Tibetans. Within two years, he was to find that an even closer acquaintance had become a target of the machinery of the Chinese security state: his wife. This led to one of the most striking of his many essays on Tibetan issues, in which he described the logic of officialdom

---

18.   See "Mainland Chinese Writer Comments on Trulku Tenzin Delek's Trial," available in translation at World Tibet News, December 7, 2002, http://www.tibet.ca/en/newsroom/wtn/archive/old?y=2002&m=12&p=7-2_3. Four of Wang's other articles on Tenzin Delek and the government's case against him can be found at http://wlx.sowiki.net//?action=index&page=3.

19.   Wang Lixiong, "Three Points of Doubt about the Case of A'an Zhaxi to Bring to the Attention of the Supreme Court for Review," January 28, 2003. Available in translation in Human Rights Watch, *Trials of a Tibetan Monk: The Case of Tenzin Delek*, 2004, Appendix VI, 95–99.

20.   Wang Lixiong, "The Time When Dharma Comes to an End," February–March 2003, available in translation at http://sotopia.net/democracy/archives/61.

in its decision to expel Woeser from her position in Lhasa in 2003. In this essay, probably for the first time in any Chinese writing on Tibet, he described China's policies as examples of cultural imperialism within its own borders.[21]

As he explored the implications of this view, Wang moved into new intellectual territory, beyond his peer group, no longer looking at China's minority peoples as specimens to be analyzed from the perspective of the center, but looking back from them to the center too. This development in Wang's thinking led some Chinese critics to accuse him of losing objectivity and turning to the right. For those of that opinion, his work in "Xizang duli luxiantu" (Roadmap to independence, 2008) would have been even more shocking,[22] for it presented a radical critique of the CCP bureaucracy responsible for handling nationalities and religion in China, and argued that the Party was incapable of solving the Tibetan issue and was instead pushing Tibetans towards seeking independence.

The sinologist Rémi Quesnel has detected in Wang's writing the ideal of the *zhinang*, the adviser who puts his knowledge at the disposal of a ruler, rather than that of a revolutionary who desires to overthrow the state.[23] This is not an accusation of accommodationism, but a reflection of Wang's rejection of the presumption, embedded in the Chinese reform movements of 1911 and 1919, that public reform cannot be achieved without overthrowing existing structures, a view that led to violence and autocracy. Wang's focus has been on constructive efforts at political change, centering on his proposal for a gradualist democratic system, and he has described his 1998 book on that topic as his major work. He has continued to develop this idea, not by creating organizations or claiming

---

21. Wang Lixiong, "Xizang mianlin de liangzong diguo zhuyi" [The two types of imperialisms that Tibet encounters: The Woeser affair in perspective], 2004, available in translation at http://wlx.sowiki.net/?action=show&id=2 and Wang and Shakya, *The Struggle for Tibet*, 115–46.

22. See http://wlx.sowiki.net//?action=show&id=321&page=1. Available in partial translation as "Independence after the March Incident," in Wang and Shakya, *The Struggle for Tibet*, 223–53.

23. Quesnel, "Wang Lixiong, an Atypical Intellectual."

a leadership position, but through peer group discussion on websites and through information-sharing networks on the internet within China.

* * *

The work of Woeser and Wang in Beijing was reshaped by events that had a major impact on all Tibetans: the protests of Spring 2008. In the years from 1987 to 1993, there had been some 200 protests by Tibetans against Chinese rule, almost all of them in Lhasa, but these had gradually diminished as policing became increasingly efficient in the Tibetan capital. In addition, in 2002, after a nine-year gap in contacts between the two sides, the Chinese authorities had formally re-opened talks with the Dalai Lama. But these talks were increasingly unproductive, with Chinese officials frequently denigrating the Dalai Lama's pleas for heightened autonomy for Tibetans. At the same time, the authorities began to extend the anti-Dalai Lama policies that they had imposed on the TAR in 1994 to the eastern Tibetan areas, even though few if any protests had occurred there in the previous two decades. A new, hardline CCP Secretary was appointed to Lhasa in 2005, leading to a sharp increase in anti-Dalai Lama rhetoric and cultural restrictions. "Patriotic education" drives were renewed in monasteries and nunneries, including, for the first time, in many monasteries in the eastern area, and the long run-up to the Beijing Olympics of August 2008 led to a stoking of ethnic Chinese nationalism across the country together with further restrictions on civic freedoms.

In March 2008, street protests abruptly resumed again in Lhasa, culminating in a major riot on March 14 in which nineteen civilians, all but one of them ethnic Chinese, were killed by protestors. A wave of about 150 incidents followed in different areas of the Tibetan plateau, involving by some estimates at least 30,000 people. Two of these resulted in the deaths of Chinese bystanders, the first significant instances of ethnic violence by Tibetans in decades; some forty or more Tibetan demonstrators are said by Tibetan sources to have been shot dead by security forces. The demands of the demonstrators seem mainly to have been for the Dalai

Lama to be allowed to return. These were milder objectives than those of the 1980s, when protestors had explicitly called for independence, but most of the new protests took place in eastern Tibetan areas outside the TAR, which had been relatively tranquil for some thirty years, and where Chinese policies had been much more relaxed than in Lhasa and the area around it. The social profile of the protestors was much wider than in the previous wave a decade earlier in Lhasa—instead of mainly monks and nuns, plus small-scale street-traders, the new demonstrations included students, farmers, and nomads as well. In other words, anti-Chinese sentiment among Tibetans had spread from the western half of the plateau to the entire Tibetan area, and from one sector of society to almost all the social classes.

Tibetan discontent was fuelled by the repeated broadcast on Chinese national television of footage showing mindless violence by some Tibetan rioters against Chinese civilians during the March 14 riot in Lhasa. The Tibetans shown in these sequences were clearly guilty of wanton violence and attempted murder, but the broadcasts, shown again and again, presented all Tibetans in a similar light, and significantly increased anti-Tibetan attitudes among Chinese people in China and abroad. They also indicated that the authorities were unlikely to take up Tibetan concerns about abusive policies in their areas. Over the following days and weeks, as demonstrations spread across Tibet, the government repeatedly denounced all protests as violent and illegal, although 80 percent of them were peaceful. This set up a vicious cycle of Tibetan demonstrations, Chinese demonization of demonstrators, and more Tibetan demonstrations. The government reacted by sending paramilitary troops into the affected areas and waging a campaign of propaganda and arrests, based on claims that the unrest had been organized by the Dalai Lama and his fellow exiles.

In March of that year, as soon as word of the first events reached Beijing, Woeser and her husband shifted from being commentators to being news-compilers. They produced daily reports on Woeser's overseas website, woeser.middle-way.net, giving detailed updates about events as they unfolded in various areas of Tibet, relayed to them by readers, blog-followers, and contacts within the affected areas. So far, none of their reports have been shown to be wrong, except for errors they themselves corrected at the time. In addition, they generally reported news without editorializing, keeping their comments and opinions for other forms of writing, such as essays and commentaries posted abroad or broadcast on Radio Free Asia, a Tibetan-language radio service based in Washington, DC. This was more or less unprecedented in the Tibetan world, and significantly increased foreign and Tibetan knowledge of what was happening within Tibet. Wang, as he had done in the attempt to defend Tenzin Delek Rinpoche, worked on mobilizing the Chinese intellectual community in a collective response to the government's hardline treatment of unrest in Tibet, and on March 22, 2008, he and some 300 signatories from within China submitted a twelve-point petition that urged the Chinese government to hold an independent investigation of the situation in Tibet.[24]

For Woeser, this attention to the collection of precise, documented information reflected a new and important addition to her work as a political and cultural commentator: she became also a researcher and a student of Tibetan history. She had already demonstrated her interest in such work two years earlier by publishing *Shajie* (Forbidden Memory: Tibet during the Cultural Revolution, 2006). This was the first detailed chronicle of the Cultural Revolution in Tibet, based on photographs of events there taken at the time by her father or his colleagues. It was followed by a second book, *Xizang jiyi* (Memories of Tibet, 2006), in which she published the texts of oral histories she had conducted with older Tibetans in Tibet, recalling their experiences of the Cultural Revolution and similar events. These were more or less the first detailed research materials about these events to appear in any language.

In 2011, Woeser resumed her role as a chronicler of events in Tibet when a new political movement emerged among Tibetans in Tibet: the

---

24.   "Twelve Suggestions for Dealing with the Tibetan Situation, by Some Chinese Intellectuals," *The New York Review of Books*, 55(8), May 15, 2008, http://www.nybooks.com/articles/21379, and Wang and Shakya, *The Struggle for Tibet*, 271–76.

practice of political self-immolation. This form of ritual suicide has long been part of Chinese cultural and political tradition, either as expressions of Buddhist piety in earlier eras, or as protests against local officials more recently. It is also found frequently as an element of political campaigning in India. But there had been no precedent for deaths by burning as a form of political expression among Tibetans, except for a political self-immolation by a Tibetan exile in India in 1998, and a single incident by a monk from Ngaba (Aba in Chinese) in the Tibetan area of Sichuan in 2009. In the twelve months from March 2011, there were twenty-two such cases, all by monks and nuns, mostly in Ngaba or neighboring prefectures. In March 2012, a second wave of public political suicides began, with some eighty self-immolations in the next twelve months, mostly carried out by young men and women who were lay people.

All of these people are said to have called for the Dalai Lama to be allowed to return to Tibet, and some left notes expressing deep fears for the future of Tibetan culture, language and education. Some also called for independence. As Wang argued in a study of these notes,[25] their protests seem to have been responses to the failure of attempts at resolution of the conflict between China and Tibetans. They also reflect the harsh measures imposed in many Tibetan areas after the unrest of 2008, and to the failure of the Chinese authorities to address earlier complaints about existing policies, especially those towards monasteries. After May 2011, Tibetans may also have been stirred to act by the decision of the Dalai Lama, then seventy-six years old, to abdicate his position as political leader of the exile government: following a long-held commitment to democratize and secularize the exile system of administration, he handed his role as political leader over to an elected prime minister, who inevitably will have less influence with Beijing.

By then, no talks had taken place between Beijing and Dharamsala for over a year, the longest gap in a decade, and anti-Dalai Lama rhetoric from Beijing had continued, perhaps leading some of the self-immolators

---

25. Wang Lixiong, "Last Words Analysis: Why Tibetans Self-Immolate?" December 17, 2012. Available in translation at http://woeser.middle-way. net/2012/12/blog-post_18.html.

to hope that their deaths might lead the Chinese leadership to resume talks with the exile leader before he dies. At the time of writing, 100 out of the 120 Tibetans who have set themselves on fire in Tibet have died in the effort to get China to allow the Dalai Lama to return and to defend Tibetan culture and religion.

In this crisis, Woeser took on another role, that of a cultural leader: expressing deep respect for the intentions of the immolators, she issued a plea, jointly with two other important cultural figures, for Tibetans to help bring the self-immolations to an end. The statement, issued in March 2012,[26] was one of the earliest such appeals, the first having been made by the Karmapa the previous November. Until the Tibetan exile government finally issued its own appeal for the immolations to end in October 2012—the Dalai Lama having declined to do so—calls from major Tibetan cultural figures for an end to the suicides came only from Tibetans like Woeser and the Karmapa who had been brought up and educated inside Tibet. It was a small but indicative marker of the difference in sensibility between Tibetan intellectuals from Tibet and those brought up in exile, a willingness to diverge from a commonly held sentiment and to take a leadership role if circumstances and reason require it.

Woeser's writings exhibit the passion of the activist and the tireless drive of the truly committed campaigner, expressed in profoundly Tibetan terms and rooted in a deeply-felt respect for religious dedication and national feeling. But her underlying decisions are carefully measured: in terms of policy outcomes, it appears that she is a pragmatist, taking the view that the Dalai Lama's proposal of a negotiated settlement leading to "a high degree of autonomy" for Tibet is a more realistic solution than seeking independence, even though it would mean

---

26.   "Call for End to Burnings: A Prominent Tibetan Writer and Two Others Appeal to Tibetans to Stop Self-Immolations," Radio Free Asia, March 8, 2008, http://www.rfa.org/english/news/tibet/burnings-03082012123141. html. See also Tsering Woeser, "Fire on the Mountain: How Many Tibetans Have to Burn Themselves before the Chinese Care?" *Foreign Policy*, March 13, 2012, http://www.foreignpolicy.com/articles/2012/03/13/ tibet_self_immolation.

remaining within the current Chinese system. This position is driven by a sense, found widely among Tibetans in Tibet and many in exile too, that the immediate challenge facing Tibetans is the need to sustain their culture, religion and identity, rather than longer-term aspirations for statehood. Wang's position is broadly similar, but is more critical of the exile administration, which he sees as having failed to respond to the immolators' implicit call, in his view, for a new approach to ending the conflict. He has called on the Tibetans to promote the method of village-level "incremental democracy" that he has advocated in his theoretical writings.[27]

Woeser's writings are generally not about the larger questions of strategy and policy that Wang has long worked on. Her focus is on bringing to light the everyday pressures faced by Tibetans and their cultural practices within China today, and explaining their inner logic as experienced by those involved. Her approach is not that of a reporter, but of a cultural commentator—she aims not to list instances of cultural loss, but to express the values that are at stake, and to communicate the feelings of Tibetans in the current crisis. It is an empathetic mode of politics and reportage, rooted in a knowledge of their history and their culture. As she put it in an interview in 2012, "I'm slowly actualizing the self-expression of a 'Tibetan identity,'" a project she described as "the biography of an entire nationality."[28] At the same time, in the vacuum of leadership created by the aging of the Dalai Lama and by the refusal of Chinese leaders to allow full discussion of their modernization policies in Tibet, she has become a leader of opinion within the wider Tibetan community, and a bridge between the inside and the outside populations. Wang, for his part, attempts similarly to focus attention through

---

27. Wang Lixiong, "Wang Lixiong: chule zifen hai neng zuo shenme?" [Except self-immolation, what else can be done?], January 14, 2012, at http://woeser.middle-way.net/2012/01/blog-post_14.html. Available in translation at Phayul, January 20, 2012, http://www.phayul.com/news/article.aspx?id=30717&t=1.

28. Pemba and Woeser, "An Eye from History and Reality."

writing on the lived experience of Tibetans, Uighurs and others under Chinese rule. Always rooted in awareness that he is neither Tibetan not Uighur, his later writing avoids claiming to know for himself what those people feel; rather, his longer aim seems to be quietly to suggest to his fellow Chinese ways in which to understand the condition and experience of non-Chinese peoples living in the PRC. Combining his ability as a narrative writer with political analysis and policy proposals, he tries to change the story that is told in China about Tibet, and to allow Tibetan and Uighur voices to be the formative, core element of that story.

Fundamentally, the Tibet issue remains what it has been ever since the British launched their pointless but provocative invasion of Tibet in 1903: a century-long attempt by Tibetans to deal with the drive of successive Chinese governments to establish their claim to Tibetan territory, alongside an effort to eradicate even the memory among Tibetans of claims to independence. But in the last two decades or more, a more immediate concern has come to the fore for Tibetans—in what form Tibetan culture and identity can survive the dual pressures of China's unifying policies and its drive for rapid modernization. It is these issues that the writings of Woeser and Wang Lixiong direct attention to, always pressing for solutions that will strengthen shared values, reconciliation and cohesion. In the coming decades, as the inhabitants of the Tibetan plateau seek meaning and direction in their lives as new, involuntary citizens of an assertive, modernizing China, the identity-building efforts of independent Tibetan intellectuals like Woeser and Chinese thinkers of the stature of Wang Lixiong will become increasingly important and decisive.

Chapter I
Old Lhasa Politicized

Freedom for Chinese, Autonomy for Tibetans

"He got the prize!"

I received this text message from a friend in Beijing, when I was on a train pulling into Lhasa on the afternoon of October 8, 2010.

Mr. Liu Xiaobo, whom we know so well, was awarded the Nobel Peace Prize.

Excited, I immediately sent his wife, Liu Xia, a congratulatory text message. Whether or not she got it is anybody's guess. By the time I got a chance to call her, her cell phone was already disconnected. So I sent this message to many of my friends—Tibetans, Hans, and foreign journalists in Beijing: "Cheers for the first ever Chinese Nobel Peace laureate."

I have known Mr. Liu for many years, but I have never addressed him as ceremoniously as I do now.

I still recall one late night when his stammering voice came through Skype to invite me to co-sign Charter 08.[1] Out of respect and trust, and the fact that he has long been concerned about the Tibet issue, I signed without any hesitation.

---

1. Charter 08 is a manifesto for human rights, democracy and rule of law, of which Liu and a few other Chinese activists were main sponsors. A clarion call to end to one-party rule, it surfaced on the Internet circa the fall of 2008 and its name invoked Charter 77 in Czechoslovakia thirty-one years before.

Not too long afterwards, Mr. Liu was taken away from his home by the authorities. And a year later, on a gloomy Christmas Day in 2009, he received a hefty sentence of eleven years.

When protests spread across the Tibetan regions in March 2008, the Communist Chinese government suppressed with a heavy hand, aggravating the situation. Liu led thirty intellectuals in China in making a twelve-point proposal to the authorities on handling the situation. The proposal garnered considerable support within the country and beyond. Following his lead, as many as three hundred Tibetologists and other scholars from around the world sent a petition, calling on then Chinese President Hu Jintao to properly resolve the Tibet issue.

In addition, Liu also penned several articles on the Tibet issue. In "The Tibet Crisis Is the Failure of Materialist Dictatorship," he said: "Blinded by materialism, the Chinese Communist Party does not see the great importance of religion to the human spirit, nor does it understand the sacred significance of the Dalai Lama to a pious people. He not only is the soul of the snow country but also the ultimate symbol of resistance of a puny people against the authoritarian Chinese regime. To have kept a pious people from their god for forty years is tantamount to depriving them of their core value. Leveling all those libelous accusations against the Dalai Lama is like gouging out Tibetans' heart with a knife."

In another article, Liu again pulled no punches: "In order to achieve Sino-Tibetan unity, Han Chinese must learn to respect Tibetans' religious belief. The best way to show respect is to allow the soul of the snow country—the Dalai Lama—to come home."

Ultimately, Liu saw how the political destinies of Hans and Tibetans intertwine. In "So Long as Han Chinese Have No Freedom, Tibetans Will Have No Autonomy," he wrote: "So long as Han people live under dictatorship, it will be unthinkable that Tibetans precede them in gaining freedom. And so long as people in China proper are denied authentic self-rule, self-rule for Tibetans and other minorities will remain a pipe dream."[2]

---

2.   Translated by Eva S. Chou, *No Enemies, No Hatred: Selected Essays and Poems* (Cambridge, MA: Harvard University Press, 2012).

And Liu came to my defense in 2004, when I was punished by the authorities for my book of essays on Tibet. He published an essay entitled "Woeser's Faith and Communist China's Atheism," in which he said: "The confrontation between a female Tibetan writer and a long-standing regime is one between freedom of faith and repression of belief, between human dignity and humiliation, and between benign belief and hardened violence.

"With its repeated intimidation, repression of religious freedom and political dissent, the Chinese Communist Party once again showed the world its vulgar, barbaric materialistic atheism."

Here, out of my deepest respect I salute Mr. Liu Xiaobo for his well-deserved Nobel Peace Prize! On an auspicious day, I shall go to a sacred temple in Lhasa and pray that he regains freedom as soon as possible.

* * *

Where Are Tibetans in the Chinese Dream?

Should we continue to place our hope on the Chinese Dream? To wit, the new Chinese president, Xi Jinping, will change his country's stance on the Tibet issue. Many people are hoping for a softening, or even constructive change.

Questions on what to expect on this issue often give me headaches. Because those who ask invariably follow up with a sentimental footnote in their retelling of the timeworn tale: That Xi's late father, Xi Zhongxun, then a high-level Chinese Communist Party official in his prime, struck up a friendship with the twenty-ish Dalai Lama. And he recalled that the elder Xi had left an impression of an enlightened gentle soul.

Now that the younger Xi has become China's most powerful man, those trying to predict how he will rule Tibet take into account not only his late father's amicable rapport with the Dalai Lama and the Tenth Panchen Lama, but also the fact that both his mother as well as his folk singer wife, Peng Liyuan, are Buddhists. Some observers even say Peng has come under the tutelage of a Tibetan Buddhist teacher. Would that not suggest she has closer ties with Tibet?

The future of Tibet should exude more than a ray of hope, so these observers keep saying.

But is that so? There is a well-known Confucian saying, "Watch one's words and then heed one's deeds." Since taking the helm last year, over and over Xi has proclaimed he would realize the great Chinese renaissance. He summed all this up as "the Chinese Dream"; reverie it is not.

"What is 'the Chinese Dream'?" Xi asked before the Chinese Communist Party congress in 2012. "To realize the great renaissance of the Chinese nation is, in my view, our nation's greatest dream in the modern era. And we're now getting closer to fulfilling this dream than ever before in our history."

In the CCP's tradition, every new leader comes into office with his own agenda. For Deng Xiaoping, it was "Reform and Opening Up." Jiang Zemin had his "Three Represents." Hu Jintao harped on "the Harmonious Society." For Xi, the Chinese renaissance should be it.

So what would the Chinese renaissance entail? For one thing, Xi's stance on Diaoyu Islands[3] seems unyielding.

Already, observers have noted how Xi has distinguished himself from his predecessors with his emphasis on the Chinese renaissance, which essentially is an expression of nationalism. The Chinese Dream, in other words, is that of a great Chinese empire. One can see no sooner has the sun set on the old imperialist nations than the upstarts rear their heads. For them, territorial sovereignty is first and foremost. They will not give up what is already under their control, and will fight tooth and nail for what is not.

Two cases in point: Since 2012, new passports issued by China are used to broadcast its claims over Taiwan, the South China Sea, and the disputed territories bordering India. And Xi commands the Diaoyu Islands Response Team, overseeing troop deployment, intelligence gathering, diplomacy and marine law enforcement.

---

3.   Known as Pinnacle Islands in the West and Senkaku Islands for the Japanese. China, Japan, and Taiwan are locked in disputes over these territories in the East China Sea.

Tibetans also have their dream: That is for the Dalai Lama to use his middle-of-the-road approach to achieve a high degree of autonomy for Tibetans, despite their growing desire for independence. However, in the eyes of Chinese leaders, even the modest middle is *de facto* independence, as intolerable as *de jure* independence. Given that sovereignty and territory are both China's core interests, the Tibetan Dream is doomed.

True that Xi has his naysayers, because there are those who deem the Chinese renaissance unattainable so long as the people are denied their heart and soul. Regardless, one thing is clear: Tibetans have no place in the Chinese Dream.

* * *

Beijing Olympics: Divided World, Divided Dream

For historical reasons, the Amdo region schedules religious ceremonies and popular festivals according to the Chinese lunar calendar. The Beijing Olympics was slated to kick off on August 8, which on the lunar calendar was the eighth day of the seventh month. That also happened to be the first day of a Buddhist ceremony at one of the county's largest monasteries, Labrang Tashi Khyil, which was to host a dance ceremony to entertain both the clerics and the laymen. Even though this tradition goes back more than two centuries, but since its timing clashed with the Beijing Olympics, officials called it off.

Crestfallen, a monk confided in me, "The government gave us a laundry list of bans: Do not leave the monastery; do not assemble; do not protest. More than a hundred plainclothes cops dressed as tourists milled about the monastery for days on end. On top of that, just about every work unit and village nearby sent their people to keep a close eye on us. Even ordinary folks had to show their IDs in order to come in and worship. Alas, if the Chinese could have their Olympics, why couldn't they let us have our ceremony?"

In protest, nearly all Tibetan store owners and restaurateurs in Labrang County (Xiahe in Chinese), home to the monastery and the historical heart of Amdo, refused to open for business on the opening day of the Games. And many old folks choked back tears as they prayed and circumambulated the monastery.

On August 12, a few days into the Olympics, it was time for the traditional horse racing festival on Sangke grassland in Gannan—an occasion for as many as 10,000 to 20,000 herders to gather and for the much-revered monks to give them blessings. In recent years, the local government has taken over the planning, turning the festival into a mélange extravaganza of trade and tourism.

Although herders had already galloped onto the grassland and pitched their tents, once the official edict came down, the festival was called off in a heartbeat.

It was easy to see why. These days, when just about every single Tibetan is treated as a potential terrorist, a gathering of more than ten thousand is inevitably seen as the greatest threat there is. It also did not help that the festival coincided with the Olympics. So local officials, who would rather not be blamed for anything that may go awry, all became disciples of the Deng Xiaoping school of nipping danger in the bud and canceled the festival.

This angered the Tibetans, which in turn put the officials doubly on guard. In the end, Xiahe was all but locked down; no one could go in or get out. Tibetans from the neighboring areas were not allowed to scooter into town, and the grassland was overrun with military police.

I interviewed some Amdo locals and asked what they thought of the Games. One of them was an old Tibetan farmer who was denounced as a rebel and sent to a labor camp in 1958, but now lives in the countryside with his children. "At first, in order to ensure smooth sailing for the Olympics, Beijing agreed to negotiate with the representative of the Dalai Lama's special envoy Lodi Gyari Rinpoche. But after two rounds the attitudes only got worse," the old farmer said. "Perhaps because once the issues over hosting the Games were resolved, Beijing could care less. This goes to show you can't take the Chinese at their word. They flip, and they flop."

A well-educated middle-aged businessman said his two children were raised in a Han-dominated city. They never realized they were different until the March 14 unrest,[4] during which they were taunted by classmates as "Tibetan separatists." This experience changed his children tremendously. When they watched the Olympics they cheered on the foreign teams and hoped to see China lose. This made the father both sad and anguished.

A monk who was detained during the unrest, and then brutally beaten, said, "Many people, not only the Tibetans but even the officials, were fearful of the Olympics, as though they were about to face off their mortal enemies on the battlefield. And the Tibetans had more to fear, not least because they were treated as enemies from the outset."

The Beijing Games were not only politicized but also drove a wedge between ethnic groups—the very opposite of the Olympic spirit. This experience will stay with all those who have suffered humiliation in the name of the Games.

* * *

The Qinghai-Tibet Railway Conscripted

The Qinghai-Tibet railway went into operation in 2006. The state-of-the-art railcars basked in media spotlight and were touted as the fruit of the collaborative efforts between Chinese and foreign investors. What is little known is that in the spring of 2008, service was suspended briefly to make way for military and munitions transport.

The military purpose of the railway was thus fully realized within two short years of it beginning operations.

---

4.   It was a series of demonstrations and protests that started in Lhasa on March 14, 2008, presumably as a recollection of the March 1959 uprising by the Tibetans against Chinese rule, but soon spread to other Tibetan areas and a number of monasteries outside the Tibet Autonomous Region (TAR). Homes and businesses were looted and eighteen civilians were killed, along with one policeman and an untold number of protesters.

At the stroke of midnight on April 25, 2008, countless armed troops escorted 675 Tibetan monks—all masked in black cloth—to Lhasa station. There, they boarded the wobbly wagons of a train bound for Golmud (Ge'ermu in Chinese), the terminus of the railway's Tibet section.

The monks were loaded on the kind of rickety trains no tourists or fortune-seeking visitors to Tibet would ever ride. When a few monks later described their ordeal, I pictured the cattle cars or freight trains in which millions of Jews were ferried to the concentration camps, and on to the crematoria.

While I would rather not tell where I met these monks, I must say this meeting was a miracle that left me beyond despondent. All I want is to tell their stories and expose Beijing's lies about religious freedom.

I was told the monks were snatched from Lhasa's Big Three monasteries—Drepung, Sera, and Gandan. Around midnight, thousands of armed Chinese soldiers barged in, followed by Tibetan police and officials serving as interpreters and accomplices. The actual number of monks arrested far exceeded the reported 675, because at Drepung alone more than 700 monks were rounded up. In addition, more than 400 were snatched from Sera, along with an untold number from Gandan.

So, what happened to those who were not among the 675 hauled off by train?

The monks murmured, "Probably they are languishing in Lhasa's jails. Who knows if they are dead or alive?"

What I know is that, of the fourteen monks who staged a sit-in at the plaza of the Jokhang Temple in March, at least one had already been sentenced to fourteen years in prison.

During detention at a makeshift military jail in Golmud, the monks were subjected to a crash course on "political education" by Tibetan teachers from Tibet University and Tibet Medical College. They schooled the monks in prohibitions and restrictions but absolutely nothing about civil rights. After three months, some of the monks were escorted back to their home province of Qinghai by local police, but they could not go home until after another round of "political education" at a local high school, and under the watch of plainclothes soldiers. After the Olympics was over in late August, those monks from Amdo and Ngaba counties were sent home under police escort like criminals. None of the monks were allowed to return to their monasteries in Lhasa.

While he was telling me all this, a monk from Sera, who called me "sister," wore a faint smile, but his face was etched with unfathomable sorrow. He said nearly all the monks fell ill in detention, and most developed a heart condition. An already-ailing twenty-two-year-old monk, Jigme Phuntsok, became sicker within twenty days, after receiving a misdiagnosis by the military doctor, and died. Another thirty-ish young monk could not bear to lie low. He banged his head against the wall and then jumped off a hospital building; he broke his neck and lost hearing in one of his ears.

Another monk who called me "sister," from Drepung, was still quite young but has already been a *geshe*, the equivalent of a master's degree in Tibetan Buddhism. He worried about his future away from the monastery. Orphaned at a tender age and has practically no family, he started his clerical career many years ago at Drepung. There are many more monks who had similar experiences.

Now as train after train files past the snow-capped Nyenchen Tanglha, it is obvious the once-mighty mountain god is rendered impotent in a regime where monks are treated as prisoners. I tried to imagine how they felt as they were being carted off in the ramshackle railcars. Truth be told, it beggared my imagination.

Police are stationed along nearly every kilometer of the long Qinghai-Tibet tracks. At the Mt. Tanggula Pass checkpoint, a police officer told me that since last year he has been watching over the tracks, which are already outfitted with a network of surveillance control devices. Nothing can escape such close watch.

* * *

The Next Big One

In the May 29, 2008 issue of *The New York Review of Books*, Robert Barnett of Columbia University and an authority on contemporary Tibet wrote: "Few predicted the intensity of recent events inside Tibet, [but] this is not true of the distinguished Chinese intellectual Wang Lixiong, [who] wrote in 1998: 'Tibet is more prosperous now than ever before in its history. However, this has not gained the PRC the allegiance of the Tibetans, more and more of whom have become attached to the Dalai Lama. . . . The current stabilization is only on the surface. One day people will riot in much greater numbers than in the late eighties.'"

So now I will continue to prophesize: Next time riots break out in Tibet, the scale will be bigger than in 2008. I can even predict when Tibet will see the next riots. If the Tibet issue sees no progress before the Dalai Lama passes away, and if he is still barred from Tibet, the moment he dies will send out the call to arms for Tibetans within China's borders.

This is not something Beijing's crackdown machinery can avert, and there is no way the government can suppress the news. Tibetans will not need to coordinate or be organized; they will all rise up spontaneously.

As anyone who understands Tibet knows, the fate of the Dalai Lama remains an open wound in the heart of every Tibetan. He is the supreme leader of Tibetan Buddhism and a living, breathing bodhisattva. He has made the ultimate sacrifice by entering into a devil's bargain: He gave up Tibet's independence in exchange for a high degree of autonomy and for the preservation of Tibetan culture and religion. For all his humility, Beijing has subjected him to endless humiliations. If he were to be barred from his homeland for the rest of his life and never again saw his people and his disciples, who have been pining for his return, the pain would be beyond words.

As long as the Dalai Lama is living, Tibetans can manage to keep their hopes alive, regardless of the ups and downs. But once he is deceased, hope becomes despair, hatred overcomes fear, and bereavement fans fanaticism. The riots at that time will be much larger in scale and scope, and tempt ever more Tibetans. And the situation surely will not calm down in a short time.

Beijing is no stranger to mass protests sparked by a leader's demise. In 1976, the mourning for the respected premier Zhou Enlai ignited unrest. And the funeral of Hu Yaobang in 1989 led to the Tiananmen Square crackdown. The only way the Chinese government can avert the next riots is to resolve the Tibet question during the Dalai Lama's lifetime, or to at least break the current stalemate.

* * *

The Fall of Lhasa

During China's reform and opening up in the 1980s, Lhasa was the destination for many talented Tibetans. I have seen quite a few young Tibetan graduates who could have remained in Beijing, Shanghai or other cities and found work there, but preferred instead to live and work in Lhasa, far from the bustle and hustle.

In the spring of 1990, I left Kham in Eastern Tibet for Lhasa, the city of my birth, to work for the Tibetan Cultural Association; some of my colleagues were from the Amdo region. At the time, Lhasa was a magnet to Tibetans. Amdo and Kham businessmen flocked here to set up their enterprises. Monks made their pilgrimage to Lhasa and studied at the Big Three monasteries in adherence to tradition. Tibetans from across the regions still regarded Lhasa as the hub. They bought houses to settle into and tried to transfer their household registration to here. Although Lhasa had all kinds of problems then, and for three years straight protests here were met with crackdowns, it still afforded more leeway and possibilities, and was relatively free and tolerant.

How things have changed since. Now two parents who come from Kham to visit their daughter married to a Lhasa local would despair at finding her living in a city at gunpoint. Soldiers rule the streets, and monks face desecration. Lhasa has degenerated from a holy city into a sin city, full of depravity and bloodshed.

Monks from outside Lhasa now must carry proof of their identity and other forms of verification in order to pass through the gauntlet of checkpoints. Rinpoches from all over the Tibetan regions steer clear of Lhasa and move to mainland China instead. Those who are already here avoid going out, living under virtual house arrest. Local monks exercise caution and try to walk the streets in casual wear as much as possible.

In the heart of Old Lhasa around the Jokhang Temple, one can often see armed police randomly stop monks or youths in Tibetan garb for interrogation and registration. Ordinary Tibetans are on guard with each other, even their own relatives, fearing there may be police informants or spies among them.

Ever fewer foreigners are visiting, and tourists are subject to numerous restrictions. Most foreign foundations and NGOs have been expelled. Tibetans entrepreneurs are either downsizing or relocating their businesses to other Tibetan regions or cities in China; even though they do not find the climate, language and way of life there agreeable, at least they can live in less fear. And since 2008, quite a few successful Tibetans have been sentenced to prison, resulting in paranoia among businessmen and entrepreneurs. No one knows what would happen tomorrow, or if they would lose the wealth they have toiled to build over the past decades to trumped-up charges. . . .

Lhasa's centripetal force on Tibetans seems to be on the wane. That is because everywhere they turn they encounter more difficulties here than elsewhere. For example, even getting a permit or a border pass for pilgrimage has become a pipe dream for many Tibetans. Although a good number of communities have been established throughout Lhasa with a lot of new homes built, many are sitting vacant. Before, Tibetans from Amdo and Kham would look to buy a house in Lhasa; now most Tibetans tend to buy properties in Chengdu, Sichuan's provincial capital. Some say as many as 200,000 Tibetans have already done so, possibly including many who refuse to live in Lhasa's shadow of fear.

No doubt Tibetans in the other provinces also face suppression, but it remains a lot more relaxed there than what goes on here. A case in point: In the summer of 2011, when I traversed the Tibetan regions from Qinghai Province to Sichuan Province, along the way I saw the long-forbidden likeness of the Dalai Lama being worshipped inside monasteries and laypeople's homes. Over the years, provincial officials have gone from strictly enforcing the ban to turning a blind eye, because they realized iron-fist enforcement would only incite greater resistance. Here in Lhasa this sort of concession is unheard of. On some of the murals that bear his image, officials have asked that a beard be painted—in order to mask the Dalai Lama and befuddle worshippers and tourists alike.

* * *

Let Go of the Dalai Lama

During the first ever online chat between the Dalai Lama and netizens in China,[5] the question that garnered the most interest was: "What are your thoughts on the two Eleventh Panchen Lamas issue?"

To wit, as another similarly popular question put it more bluntly: "After you pass away, the Chinese Communist Party is bound to appoint your successor. What is your countermeasure?"

"I think the Dalai Lama as an institution does not matter much. The Chinese Communist Party cares a lot more about it than I do," said the Dalai Lama, with a laugh. "So, it is likely that the two-Panchen phenomenon will arise. And when it does, it'll only add to the confusion and not help the situation."

The Dalai Lama's response shows he has foreseen the prospect of dueling Dalai Lamas succeeding him, and that it will spell chaos. The Chinese government is not the least bit concerned, because chaos is conducive to its divide-and-rule strategy over the Tibetans. Therefore, creating chaos could be precisely its intent.

So how would the Dalai Lama contend with the chaos?

"In 1969, I made a very formal announcement," said the Dalai Lama, "that we should let the people of Tibet decide whether or not to continue with the institution of the Dalai Lama. Similarly, in 1992, I've made a formal declaration that once the Tibet issue is resolved, I won't serve in

---

5.   The chat, which Wang Lixiong helped run, took place in May 2010.

any position in the Tibetan government. All Tibet-related affairs will be managed by the civil servants who remain in Tibet. And since 2001, the head of the Tibet Government in Exile has been democratically elected by Tibetan exiles to a five-year term."

We can see that in the Dalai Lama's mind, the easiest way to deal with the two Dalai Lamas chaos is to diminish the institution's importance to Tibet, and to make the democratized Tibetans the masters of their future and of their destiny.

In other words, the Dalai Lama saw the key to solving the problem. That is why in his remaining years he is focusing his efforts on democratizing the Tibetan society. However, even though Tibetan exiles have made great strides on the road to democracy, little has changed in the status quo that places the Dalai Lama at the center of their universe.

The democratically elected parliament and chief executive are far from being the Dalai Lama's surrogates. In the long run, it is going to take more efforts to explore and establish a democratic system in order to realize his ideal.

* * *

Tibetans Are Ruined by Hope

In Tibet, there is a saying at the tip of every tongue: "Tibetans are ruined by hope; Chinese are ruined by suspicion." Tibetans often say this in self-ridicule, helplessly, hopelessly, or heedlessly. Although they talk the talk with a cauldron of emotions, they continue to lose themselves in a reverie of hope about the future.

The world-renowned Tibetologist, Melvyn Goldstein of Case Western Reserve University in Ohio, whose research on both historical and contemporary Tibet has been widely published, recently co-authored a biography entitled *A Tibetan Revolutionary: The Political Life and Times of Bapa Phüntso Wangye*.[6] Once I opened the book, I found this saying in

---

6.   Berkeley: University of California, 2004.

the epigraph of the latest work by this scholar, who has spent his career examining the complicated and entwined history of the Chinese and the Tibetans.

Does this saying not hammer home the book's thesis? In other words, does this saying not encapsulate the struggles of Phunwang's life? He was one of the first Tibetans who put their faith in Communism and also among the first to have collaborated with the People's Liberation Army to "liberate" Tibet. Some now say he should not have brought the Communist fox to the chicken coop. But anyone who understands the ideals and aspirations of Phunwang and his contemporaries should know they struggled not for their own gains, but for the greater good of Tibet.

In 2004, Phunwang, already well into his eighties, penned two important letters—one to Chinese president Hu Jintao; the other to the general director of the China Tibetology Research Center and state-appointed Tibetan spokesman Lhagpa Phuntshogs. In his letters, Phunwang urged Beijing to have a dialogue with the Dalai Lama as soon as possible and to allow him to return to his homeland. Phunwang stressed, again and again, that this issue concerned not just the long-term harmony and sustainable development of the Tibetan regions, but also the unity and equality, survival and prosperity of all ethnic groups. Yet, his plea fell on deaf ears. Does this not represent one of the myriad dreams harbored by the Tibetans?

Not long before, I met a Tibetan couple who had settled overseas but visited Lhasa recently. They resented the increasing sinicization of Tibet, but that was not what they found the most disturbing. They were most concerned about those Tibetans, having been co-opted by the regime, who are preoccupied with material pursuit and enjoyment and mired in complacency.

Beijing and the Tibetan Government in Exile had already had five rounds of talks, the couple recalled with much sadness. As there appeared to be a breakthrough, the exile government asked all Tibetans to cease their protests and demonstrations against China. Most of them heeded the call, patiently waiting for the situation to improve. But things have only gone downhill since then, against Tibetans' wishes: The CCP leadership in Tibet declared it was in "mortal combat" with the Dalai Lama.

And the Chinese border guards shot dead a group of fleeing Tibetan pilgrims on the Nangpa La pass near the Nepal-Tibet border in 2006. Clearly, our dreams were once again shattered.

True that Tibetans have too many dreams, and they should not carry on dreaming. Perhaps it is only when dreams are dashed will there be a real breakthrough.

* * *

From Self-Immolation to Self-Rule

Without reservation, I respect all those Tibetans who have set themselves on fire.[7] Although not every one of them has accomplished their goal, and regardless of whether or not they have any clear intent, their collective impact lies in fueling the courage of a people.

For the underdog in particular, courage is a precious resource; more often than not it turns the tables. Self-immolation calls for enormous courage. And it was with courage of an earth-shattering and awe-inspiring kind that the first sixteen Tibetans perished on Chinese soil in self-immolation, culminating with that of Sobha Rinpoche of Golok, in Amdo. I think the goal of working up the courage of the Tibetan people has been accomplished.

So now the question is: What should such precious courage be harnessed for? Carrying on with self-immolations and burning off courage would become too much of a waste from this point on, I believe.

The courage inspired by these martyrs should be used to produce real results. And herein lie their hopes, as well as the value of their sacrifice.

That said, self-immolation still is a form of violence, extreme violence, only that it is done to oneself. Inflicting violence on oneself, other than in desperate protestation or as a last-ditch effort to defend one's dignity, stems from the hope for real impact.

---

7.   Between March 2011 and August 2013, more than 120 self-immolations
      were reported.

Just as Dr. Martin Luther King Jr. once said, "We shall match your capacity to inflict suffering by our capacity to endure suffering. . . . But ye assured that we will wear you down by our capacity to suffer. One day we shall win freedom, but not only for ourselves. We shall so appeal to your heart and conscience that we will win you in the process . . ."[8]

The realization of such hopes is predicated on the existence of conscience. The machine of an authoritarian regime, however, is grounded only on rigid structure and ruthless logic, as well as bureaucratic interests. In 1989, when thousands of young people in Tiananmen Square were on the verge of death from hunger strike, who got any glimpse of the regime's conscience?

Here lies the limitation of past nonviolent struggles: The outcome is determined not by the resistance but by the regime. The resistance can only apply pressure, but as long as the regime does not give an inch there can be no progress. The tough position in which Tibet now finds itself is inevitable.

So, where is the north star that points the way out of the woods for Tibet? This is a question that, I feel, demands an answer first and foremost. A people who do not know their way can only go about blindly; even such heroic sacrifices as self-immolations can make many people feel ever more desperate. After every self-immolation, emotions stir and arguments rage to no avail.

It would be unfair to say the martyrs have shown much courage but little wisdom. Wisdom is not the cleverness to lie low and stay alive, but the foresight to lead Tibet out of the conundrum. Although that is not something ordinary people should or can undertake, attributing all wisdom to only the Dalai Lama, who has bowed out of politics, is irresponsible. He has already affirmed the principle of nonviolence and the middle-of-the-road course. It is up to the politicians to show the wisdom.

Yet, there has been very little of that. Beijing is waving wads of cash in one hand and brandishing the butcher's knife in the other. Assuming the Tibetan Government in Exile speaks for the other side, it is unclear besides making statements its representatives know what else to do.

---

8. *Strength to Love* (New York: Fortress Press, 1963), 40.

Please tell the brave Tibetans what they can do. If they know, more of them will choose life over self-immolation and the short-lived media attention it garners.

In my view, village self-rule is Tibet's way out. Through the participation of each ordinary villager, the villages could govern themselves. The masses become active participants, no longer passive observers of the endless and fruitless negotiations, or chips in the high-stake political games between Beijing and Dharamsala.

Genuine self-rule should sprout from the grassroots, from the bottom to the upper echelons, with autonomy at every level, all the way for the entire Tibetan regions. As long as grassroots autonomy serves as the starting point, a future of regional autonomy is nigh.

The latest exemplar was in Wukan, Guangdong Province. As Wukan's villagers rose up against illegal land grabs by party officials, they threw in the towel and fled. Each clan elected its own representative, and the representatives voted for members to form the village council. The autonomous council brought not only order to village affairs but also the authorities to the negotiation table, even in the midst of government suppression and a siege by paramilitary troops.

Can Tibetan villagers achieve similar success? Tibetan villages are not lacking in the conditions found in Wukan. Once a village succeeds, Tibetans will have an example to follow. When ten more succeed, the end of the tunnel would be near. When a hundred rise up, a truly autonomous Tibet would become within reach.

I know a familiar refrain from the skeptics: What Hans can do Tibetans cannot; they will face separatism charges and suppression, and so on. But for too long we have given in to all these doubts. The answer is a single question: If you are not afraid of setting yourself on fire, what else can scare you?

A people's courage is certain to be the talisman of their triumph.

Chapter II
Economic Imperialism with Chinese Characteristics

Winners and Losers under Tibet's Capitalism

The market economy is gradually taking hold in Tibet. Some of my Tibetan friends see in it a crisis that has made them ever more anxious: Han Chinese are taking away their jobs, not by brute force but through the might of the market. In the marketplace, the rule is the survival of the fastest. So long as they prove themselves to be more efficient than the Tibetans, the Hans streaming into Tibet take over the market.

For example, it takes a Tibetan tailor more than two weeks to sew a Tibetan costume; a Han tailor takes only two to three days. To build a house, Tibetans ask for as much as a year, plus gifts; Hans take no more than two to three months to finish the job and play by market rules.

When a Tibetan friend of mine was getting a house built in suburban Lhasa, he hired some of the poorest villagers to cut stones. These stone-cutters drank on the job and could hardly stay sober or awake. The stones they produced were too fragile to build with, but they still demanded to be paid.

However much my friend wanted to support his own people, he ended up hiring Hans. Such is the reality of the market.

These days in Lhasa, Han workers nearly dominate auto repair, cobbling, construction, farming, and so on. Even the majority of cabbies and pedicab drivers are Hans. In and around the Barkor, most of the Tibetan-style furniture comes from Han carpenters. The Hans are even employed in such traditional trades as sewing prayer cushions, sculpting Buddha statues, and preparing Tibetan meals. No wonder this saying is going around in Lhasa: "There is no job the Hans won't take, except lamas and sky burial masters."

Many Tibetans are worried they would lose not only their livelihoods but also their homes. Quite a lot of Tibetans have leased their state-granted apartments to Hans. Living on rental income and not having to work—a comfortable life while it lasts. But such complacency does not cultivate competitiveness. One day when Tibetans find themselves in a pinch, they might have to sell their house to Hans.

These days, few local Tibetans have remained on the Barkor. As one of the symbols of Old Lhasa, it is changing gradually but palpably.

Some pessimistic Tibetans lament that soon enough they will be at the mercy of the Hans.

* * *

Public Square or Propaganda?

Modern-day imperialism no longer flexes its muscles by simply occupying land or plundering treasure. What has emerged more and more often is what the late Edward Saïd called "cultural imperialism."

Cultural imperialists show their solipsistic conceit by flaunting their civilization as the one and only—and the superior. And they see themselves as the benefactor of what in their eyes the lesser peoples.

An epitome of such imperialistic hubris is the Taizhou Square in Chushur (Qushui in Chinese) County, along the main road to Lhasa from the nearest airport.

Taizhou is a city in Jiangsu Province, roughly 130 miles from Shanghai and the hometown of former Chinese president Hu Jintao.[1] In the name of "aiding" Tibet, Taizhou's officials poured large sums of money into

---

1. As Chinese Communist Party Secretary for Tibet in 1988, Hu Jintao called in the paramilitary troops and then the military to suppress the protests there. Hu was president from 2003 to 2012.

building the eponymous square; it has helped few Tibetans in any meaningful way.

The square, which takes up enormous space, is fashioned entirely in Chinese style. With its traditional pavilion and a small arched bridge, it looks oddly out of place. In the middle stands a metal frame supporting a gigantic stainless steel ball, meant to be a symbol of mainstream ideology of science and progress. Panels plastered with the likenesses of the CCP leaders and political slogans ring the square. Ideological propaganda, pure and simple.

It is obvious whoever designed the square had little thought about Tibetans and their culture. Other than taking up huge tracts of farmland, the square has very little to do with the locals. It is no exaggeration to say the square was not built with human users in mind.

I once took a walk on the square; I felt as though I were treading on a frying pan. The cement-paved ground reflected the sunlight painfully into my eyes. The few grassy lawns around were fenced off, guarded by "Do Not Enter" signs. The faux flowing creek in the center offered little relief, because the water far down was hardly reachable.

The expansive square has only two stone benches. Far apart and with hardly any shade, they are more like symmetrical sculptures than comfortable seating.

It was as soulless as a public square could get. The wide streets nearby were also deserted. The entire place was a ghost town, even though I was there on a Sunday.

Taizhou Square was built by the imperialists to realize their physical and cultural dominion, and to flaunt their wealth. Perhaps the designers had hoped Tibetans would be so in awe as to kowtow to such a gesture of subjugation.

Yet the locals responded with a collective shrug. And the square sits there like an extravagant ruin.

* * *

The Pernicious Fungus Economy

The prices for caterpillar fungi,[2] prized ingredients in traditional Chinese medicine, just keep soaring. Now a catty (1.3 lbs) can command as much as 40,000 to 50,000 yuan. In most cases, they are sold by the piece. A nice one can fetch seventy or even up to a hundred yuan. In the Tibetan areas where the fungi grow, a family spending a month digging for them can rake in 20,000 yuan during the harvesting season. They can build a house or buy a car—all on fungus income.

Since the fungi have become so valuable that they can help pay for anything people dream of, they are also things people are fighting over. A tiny twig of the fungus can spark a swirl of armed fighting, killing, cheating and robbing everywhere. Villagers barricade their land and violently chase out all those who encroach. Even relatives turn mortal enemies and lifelong friendships dissolve into bloodbaths. All these have become common occurrences.

Compared with fungus harvesting, farming or herding seems too much work for too little. One long year of labor pales in the face of a few twigs of fungi. So some Tibetans no longer bother to toil in the field or to herd cattle. Even the traditional crafts passed down through generations have fallen by the wayside. Except during the month when they go all out to dig for fungi, these Tibetans lounge about for the rest of the year, twiddling their thumbs.

With all that free time to kill, these Tibetans turn to other pastimes, as the saying goes: "Those who have made a fortune seek pleasure." So even the remotest of towns like Gonjo (Gongjue in Chinese) see many more cafes and wine bars, teeming with prostitutes both local and from the mainland. Even monasteries nestled in the mountains are no match for the spread of desire and decadence. What before was pristine becomes corrupt, and the temples grow ever more spectacular and luxurious. Living Buddhas cruise in cars worth a million yuan; some monasteries are retrofitted with elevators.

---

2.   The fungus is a medicinal ingredient highly prized by practitioners of traditional Chinese medicine.

When even the monks are distracted or abandon their studies altogether, there are bound to be conflicts and problems inside the monasteries. If even the clerics are powerless to counter such challenges, ordinary folks fare much worse.

Life, however, has not improved with the growing wealth. Those who now own cars and color TVs find themselves worse off. A friend recalls one such family from his hometown. The wife and the daughter lavish on lipsticks and hair gel, but there are hardly cows or goats in the backyard. The family has got fourteen broken scooters laying about the front of the house. When a scooter rider from out of town stopped by, thinking that it was a repair shop where he could get his tire patched up, the family offered him an old tire—in return for his shoes. There was not a pair of good shoes around the house.

The old-timers who have seen it all cannot help but rue these vicissitudes. In the past, whenever there was a death, everyone in the village would light the yak butter lamp and mourn the deceased. Now, whenever visitors come through town, everyone wants to take advantage of them.

* * *

The "Nineteenth Army"

Most of the sex workers in Tibet hail from mainland China.

These women just keep streaming in. Locals call them the "Nineteenth Army," after the Eighteenth, the branch of the People's Liberation Army deployed to occupy Tibet more than a half-century ago.

Prostitution has seeped into every town and village in the Tibetan regions. Sichuanese hookers would barter with country shepherds looking for sex for two or three twigs of caterpillar fungi. A twig fetches no more than fifty yuan in the countryside.

But then there are also prostitutes who come from the ranches and villages in Tibet. They are known to be the most down-market and cheapest of all, and would deal, reportedly, for a two-yuan bowl of Tibetan noodles.

A Tibetan friend told me this story. Once in Tibet, some tourists from mainland China are hell-bent to look for Tibetan prostitutes. For some, this is desire driven by curiosity. Then there are those who have succumbed to the ludicrous lore: Having sex with Tibetan women can cure arthritis.

More often than not, patrons like them do not have the nerve themselves to seek out the Tibetan ladies of the night. Since many Han women have dressed up as Tibetans, there is no telling who is the real deal, unless one knows the local tongue.

This is where Tibetan-speaking tourist guides come in. My friend happens to know a female Tibetan guide who can come to aid. Of course anyone can see this is not the right thing to do, but this Tibetan guide could hardly resist the wad of cash a Han big-spender dangled in her face. As she went looking, she ran into her grade school classmate, working as a hooker.

Both women were very embarrassed by the nature of the transaction that brought about this brief reunion. A deal was made, nonetheless. Of the 2,300 yuan her client splurged on the procurement, the guide gave her classmate 600 yuan—a fairly good price for one night. But everything ended there: Both women have gone out of their way to avoid running into each other again.

* * *

Tibetan Women Marry Han Chinese as a Way Out

On the train from Lhasa to Shanghai, I shared a compartment with a young married Tibetan woman who hailed from Dechen Tibetan Autonomous Prefecture in Yunnan Province, just over the river from TAR. She had come to Lhasa to visit her parents on pilgrimage and was heading back to Yangzhou in Jiangsu Province on the coast. There, she led a dance troupe of Tibetan girls who performed at entertainment venues and for special events, such as opening ceremonies and celebrations. She netted about seven to eight thousand yuan a month. But her brother, she said, sang at a Lhasa nightclub and could make a thousand yuan on a single night.

Like many in their hometown, the brother and sister quit school after a few years to help their parents make ends meet. Every year, they would trek around the mountains for caterpillar fungi and matsutakes, but like many Tibetans the ability to sing and dance runs in their blood. In the late 1990s, when mainland Chinese in the entertainment business set their sight over the remote Tibetan regions, they spotted many pretty young faces. These Tibetans had grown up singing and dancing; they were stage-ready performers with an exotic air. So the brother and sister were recruited by a commercial troupe and traveled to Hainan Island, Beijing, and Tianjin to perform.

Within a few years, it dawned on them they were getting only a tiny slice from their boss's fat pie. In this business, what they are selling is youth, so how can they carry on when they get old? They realized they should become their own boss. So they went home and recruited other Tibetan girls to form a dance troupe. With a few years of experience, the brother and sister had built rapports all over. The troupe traveled to Inner Mongolia, and later performed in Xinjiang and the Northeast. And since last year it has made Yangzhou its base. These days, her brother is back singing in Lhasa; the sister married a Han, and the couple has started their own troupe.

Other than visiting her parents, she never goes back to her hometown again, but lives with her husband far from the Tibetan regions. Of the nine girls from her village, six had married Hans. I asked her why. She said Tibetan guys are handsome, but they love to drink, gamble and have fun—not the type one should settle down with.

Last year, when she returned to her village, nearly all the young people had left to find work in the city, leaving only the old folks to till the land. Once they have lived in the city for a while, young people are unwilling to go back to the country.

"What about the young girls you've recruited to perform in the city?" I asked. "What will they do when they're too old to dance any longer? What lies ahead for them?"

She scarcely knew, she said, and could not wrap her mind around it. She said a lot of the girls from her hometown had gone to perform for rich Han men at dinner to jazz things up. Sometimes, these men would shower the girls with tips and ask them to drink with them.

She did not allow her dancers to moonlight for tips, she said, for fear that they would easily become unchaste. If that happens, how can she face their parents?

The best way out for these girls, I gathered, is to find a Han husband in the city, just like what she did.

Finally, she said she was nostalgic about the time before she left home: She and her folks had little money, yet they were happy.

Those days were gone forever. At that thought her eyes welled up.

* * *

Merchants of Fake Culture

The charlatan merchants on the Barkor apparently are highly adept in the art of deception, and they excel in the game of selling Tibet. They have pulled wool over the eyes of many of those interested in Tibetan culture, giving the region a bad reputation. How despicable!

In Lhasa, a shopping center called Top Peak Tibetan Artwork reportedly was founded by two Sichuanese brothers, along with their business partner from northern China, who later was cheated out of the partnership. The brothers operate the business with a bagful of tricks, all serving to help customers part with more of their money. For example, the shop would have two of the same Buddha statues—one for display, the other stashed in the cellar. When tourists are herded to the shopping center by their tour guide, the brothers would tell the tourists what they are looking at is a fake, thus piquing their curiosity enough to inquire about the real thing. Then the brothers would say they have got the real thing, too, on consignment from monasteries that are raising money for renovation. The tourists would be led down to the cellar to see the "authentic" statue. Those who want to buy it have to register their name and address. That

Figure 1

On guard for self-immolations, firefighters and police officers insert themselves into a ceremony at the Sera Monastery.

Figure 2

The omnipresence of police in Tibetan celebrations.

Figure 3

A catchpole at the ready to restrain anyone attempting a self-immolation.

Figure 4

Around Lhasa, countless surveillance cameras keep watch at all major temples.

Figure 5

Paramilitary troops remained camped in the Khampa region in Qinghai Province even a few months after the 2008 unrest.

Figure 6

Helicopters have become part of the skyline of a Lhasa under lockdown.

Figures 7 and 8

The bounty of mineral resources surrounding Lhasa is being exploited at the expense of Tibetans' well-being. Drinking water is contaminated.

way, the brothers would tell the tourists, the monasteries can be assured the statues land in the good home of decent people.

So, hook, line and sinker, the tourists plunk down a lot more cash for what they think is the real deal, paying a hundred to a thousand times the wholesale price. Once, the brothers even managed to sell something that had cost eight yuan for as much as twenty thousand yuan.

Another trick is to recruit Tibetans to weave carpets on the spot. These carpet weavers are paid a few hundred yuan a month to churn out a carpet in two weeks to be used in a bait-and-switch. The shopping center then passes off machine-made-in-China products as handwoven artisan carpets for much higher prices.

The other day, I was at the shopping center and spotted a sign near the entrance that read in Tibetan, Chinese and English: Collection Drive for China Lhasa SOS Children's Home. I had a hard time believing that was for a bona fide charity. If someone was using Tibetan orphans for scams, that was truly unforgivable.

To be sure, cheats are not confined to this shopping center. On my blog, a Tibetan living in a Western country left this comment: "Every time I chat with my Western friends, they would describe to me, in great disillusionment, how they were duped by 'the Tibetans.' Before they set foot there, Tibet in their mind is sacred, a paradise on earth. But once there, especially in Lhasa, they felt as though they were caught up in a con game." This blogger went on: "It broke my heart to look into their eyes, so saddled with disappointment. That's why I never suggest to those who admire Tibet that they should check out Lhasa or other Tibetan regions. I fear they'd be cheated all the same. I fear they'd come away convinced that Tibet is one big 'con game.'"

But indeed, too many people are making a living out of selling Tibet. Not too long ago, when I was wandering about on the Barkor, I ran into someone I had met years ago in Chengdu, the capital of Sichuan Province. Back then, he was a dealer in Tibetan art.

When I asked what he was doing these days, he declared smugly, "Same old, same old, still promoting Tibetan culture."

* * *

Only State-Sanctioned Tour Guides Need Apply

The campaign against Tibetan tour guides was sparked by a letter in 2002 from a Canadian Chinese in the tourism business who happened to have traveled to Tibet. He wrote to Beijing and reported that the Tibetan guides would tell the tourists the People's Liberation Army were "Chinese troops sent from the mainland." These guides also explained that some temples had been defaced during the Cultural Revolution. Even the guides' "inappropriate" look during a flag-raising ceremony at the Potala Palace—a sure sign of their pro-independence bent—became a reportable offense. The complainer even went so far as to note that most of the Tibetan guides had returned from India and tended to side with the Dalai Lama, thus threatening Chinese sovereignty over Tibet.

This letter of complaint reached the highest echelon of the central government: Then-Chinese president Hu Jintao personally issued an edict to purge all Tibetan guides who had come home from India. And a guide named in the letter was thrown into jail.

It is true that many guides studied in India; they spoke good English and were familiar with other cultures. So they proved popular with travel agencies. After these guides were gone, Tibet faced a serious shortage. Beijing came to rescue with a "Help Tibet" campaign. Every year, the tourism profession would deploy guides from the mainland provinces to work in Tibet.

The influx of these Han guides put tour agencies between a rock and a hard place. That is because foreign tourists generally are unwilling to have Hans as their guides in Tibet. Those who are tactful would explain: Just as they want Han guides rather than Tibetans to show them the mainland, they prefer Tibetan guides while touring Tibet. The more adamant foreigners refuse to join the tour unless they get a Tibetan guide.

The "Help Tibet" guides have fairly good foreign language skills and decent work attitudes, but they do not understand Tibet's history and culture. All they can do is go by the book, and take care to follow party lines on politically sensitive matters. For instance, at the Potala and the Norbulingka palaces, the guides must make sure to say that the Dalai

Lama instigated a revolt, had to flee his motherland, and so he deserves a life in exile.

Such propaganda irks many foreign tourists, but their Han guides insist they are simply hewing to the facts. Confrontations often result in heated arguments, or even clashes.

With the completion of the Qinghai-Tibet railroad, Beijing is about to embark on ambitious plans to expand tourism in Tibet. The issue of non-native guides will escalate. Tourism does not thrive on hotels and rail service alone; the human factor matters. Western tourists, or even Han ones, prefer to be shown around by Tibetan locals rather than Han transplants. This much is clear, even to the Han guides in Tibet.

So they give themselves Tibetan names, learn the Tibetan tongue, wear Tibetan costumes and pretend to be Tibetan. When they are exposed by foreigners who speak Tibetan, these phonies muddle through by claiming that they are part-Tibetan, part-Han.

What Beijing needs to understand is: Tourists come all the way to Tibet not to get an earful of party propaganda—but to see Tibet with their own eyes.

* * *

Railroad to Perdition

Few railroads garnered the constant attention and variety of comments that the Qinghai-Tibet railway did. Beijing formally brought it on line in 2006 on the anniversary of the CCP's founding, thus signaling the railway's political significance. Afterwards, fanned by the media frenzy, Chinese masses deluged Tibet. The TAR Tourism Bureau reported that within twenty days nearly ninety thousand Chinese filled the train cars. Lhasa was choked with visitors and became seriously overcrowded. The locals saw their daily life disrupted: Prices for staples, vegetables and meat shot up, and the monasteries were packed with tourists. All these caused Tibetans to grumble endlessly.

Tibetans have mixed feelings about the railway. Six months after its opening, in January 2007, I made a point of riding the train from Beijing to Lhasa. I found only a few tourists on board in this off-peak season, but there were many Tibetan students heading home for the winter break. They started boarding school in mainland China when they were little. Back then, it cost an arm and a leg to travel back and forth, so for many years they could not go home for the Tibetan New Year. The affordable fare of the new train is an antidote to homesickness. Another benefit of the railway is that now it is easier for Buddhists to crisscross a large swath of the Tibetan regions and even to travel to mainland China on pilgrimage.

The staff I met on the train told me the railway does not serve any economic purpose, only political and military objectives. While Tibetans may see no economic value in it, many Chinese businessmen and workers regard the railroad as the path to Tibet's mineral riches. According to official statistics, more than 2,500 potential mining sites have been discovered in TAR, i.e. thirty-some mining sites for each of the seventy-six counties. "Gold diggers" from mainland China have already descended upon Tibet along the rail line, all bent on exploring, excavating, and trading mining rights. The nightmare that the Tibetan highlands' fragile ecosystem will be destroyed is becoming a reality.

But if you ask Chinese officials and their anointed scholars, they will shrug off those concerns and counter with this bald-faced defense: We want the Tibetan people to enjoy their right to modernization.

Tradition and modernization—both are indispensable. Taken at face value, this seems to make sense. But what is most important to Tibet is not modernization but meaningful autonomy. Besides, what is modernization, really? What is unfolding in Tibet is pseudo-modernization, essentially a kind of invasion, a sugar-coated, disguised act of violence. As a people without autonomy, we must tell between different kinds of invasion.

In truth, the problem does not lie with the railroad. If Tibet could have real autonomy, then not just one single railroad, but even a railroad in every village would be under Tibetan control. Without autonomy, Tibetans have no say over their destiny and can only see their rights usurped by others. They become marginalized in their homeland, denied the benefits that are being exploited by the "gold diggers."

Without autonomy, Tibetans will not see the blissful bright future that Chinese officials have claimed the Qinghai-Tibet railway would bring. Worse still, it could prove to be the railroad to perdition for Tibetans.

* * *

Riding the Train to Lhasa

The Qinghai-Tibet railcars were packed with tourists from all over China. The timeworn song "Riding the Train to Lhasa" kept playing over and over.

Looking a bit uneasy, a civil servant from Hubei Province in central China asked me: "How safe is it in Tibet?"

"It's very safe," I said, "for *your* people."

Seated next to me, the few youngsters who had been chatting in the Beijing dialect listened up, and asked why.

"Well, on the streets paramilitary troops and plainclothes police are everywhere," I replied.

The civil servant was empathetic, "Don't Tibetans find it very uncomfortable?"

"That has something to do with the few Tibetans who have set themselves on fire, doesn't it?" one of the youngsters raised his voice, butting in. It looked like some people have heard of the self-immolations after all, even though the CCP's propaganda arm scarcely mentioned them and has banned all public discussion.

I gave them a good hard look, as though they were from a different planet. "Not just a few. Already more than fifty Tibetans have done that, from all over the Tibetan area, as well as in exile," I replied.

Although we all were speaking the same language, I felt I had hit a roadblock in our exchange. Self-immolation is by no means a rare tragedy. But those from a different culture may understand selfish actions far more readily than selfless acts. Even so, I was eager to keep our conversation going, by describing the last words of those Tibetans who chose to perish in flames. Yet, it seemed none of my fellow passengers was willing to hear anymore.

Touring Tibet, after all, is the dream of many Chinese. Although now many forms of transportation afford them easy access, these tourists never seem to get their fill during their vacations of two weeks or less. All they focus on is the scenery, as well as the "Tibet attractions" touted by travel agents. They could care less about the locals, not least those self-sacrificial Tibetans.

The Buddha teaches that all living beings are equal. In reality, however, the treatment received by different ethnic groups is like night and day. When the teeming train pulled into Lhasa, the dozen or so Tibetans aboard were all held by paramilitary troops. I presented my I.D. card to one of the police officers, who swiped it through a device like a credit card reader.

"Woeser," he announced loudly, "stay there."

All non-Tibetan passengers, meanwhile, breezed through the checkpoint, extremely excited about charging into every corner of Lhasa. Even those afflicted by altitude sickness regained their energy.

So what became of those detained Tibetans? They were all taken to a police station near the depot. The two middle-aged Tibetans who had come from Qinghai Province without an entry permit were sent home. Their plea with the officers, all fellow Tibetans, fell on deaf ears. Those with an entry permit still had to have their identification papers photocopied, state their reasons for coming to Lhasa and register a local address. Before they could be released, they had to print their name and sign with a blood-red palm print.

When two young people from Amdo and I walked out of the police station, they sighed, "We're Tibetans, but it's so hard for us to get into Lhasa." And their voice choked.

Chapter III
Religion under Siege

Cassock vs. Police Uniform

The violence that broke out on Lhasa's streets in March 2008 was to a large extent triggered by paramilitary troops beating peacefully protesting monks. This was so nearly a replay of the Lhasa incident in 1987 that it was shocking to see officials never learn their lessons.

That has everything to do with their attitude toward monks. In the eyes of the officials, monks are parasites that live on handouts. They buttress the Dalai Lama's base of support in Tibet and fuel Tibetans' desire for independence. They are troublemakers and instigators who pose a threat to the regime. All in all, they are bad news.

For all the appearances of religious freedom the authorities are trying to keep up, deep down they regard monks with disdain and disgust. Once faced with challenges from monks, the authorities react reflexively with violence.

On the contrary, as the traditional intelligentsia in Tibetan culture and one of the Three Treasures of Tibetan Buddhism, monks command an exalted position in Tibetans' hearts, highly revered as spiritual guides and protectors. That is why no Tibetan can stand seeing monks humiliated and tortured. Any violent act by the authorities against monks inevitably touches off unrest. Only those blinded by the hubris of power would fail to see such consequences.

Not only have the authorities failed to reflect on their conduct, but they have even made things worse. After the unrest, monks everywhere were targeted; many well-respected monasteries were subject to humiliating searches by military police. Besides rounding up those monks who had participated in the protests, the authorities placed countless others under house arrest. Some monasteries were shuttered, and monks who had relocated from other provinces were banished from Lhasa. All the monasteries were ordered to roll out a "patriotic education" campaign, forcing their monks to publicly denounce the Dalai Lama. Many monks decided to avoid this ordeal by fleeing, leaving some monasteries without a single soul.

Before the unrest, it is safe to say quite a few monks were political agnostics preoccupied only with learning Buddhist teachings. Their discontent was confined to Beijing's policies, and they were not opposed to Chinese rule wholesale. But the crackdown has since impelled them to reflect more deeply on Tibet's political future, nudging ever more of them to support independence.

There is a Tibetan folk song that describes a monk like this: "Whether I stand up or stumble, I live by a stick of incense. Nothing covers my forehead but a clutch of hair; nothing over my behind but a piece of rag." Free from the tethers of family ties and with nothing to lose, monks are fearless in their resistance and defiance. That is also why historically they spearheaded uprisings.

So once monks are backed into the corner, the authorities have set themselves up with the toughest of opponents. And given the reverence Tibetans have for monks and the fact they circulate among laypeople, the monks' antipathy to Chinese rule and their desire for independence will not remain insulated. Their influence is sure to spread far and wide.

* * *

Framing Monks as Terrorists

Not too long ago, Chinese authorities announced that police had uncovered a stash of weapons in Kirti Monastery in Ngaba County (Aba in Chinese), Sichuan Province. They found 6 small-bore rifles, 14 guns of all kinds, 498 bullets, 4 kilograms of explosives and 33 prohibited knives.

All these were proof, local police said, that the monks were engaged in violence. More recently, inside a monastery in Gannan Prefecture of Gansu Province, police have seized a trove of guns and ammunitions. The police will continue to find similar "evidence," it would seem, in the monasteries across the Tibetan regions.

Anyone familiar with Tibetan monasteries knows where those weapons are placed. In every monastery there is a shrine for a *dharmapala*, protector of the law in Tibetan Buddhism, and every shrine has some weaponry simply hoisted from the center pillar. Some are antiques, such as bows and arrows that have been passed down through generations and are symbolic of the safeguarding of gods. Other weapons are dedicated by career hunters or those involved in grassland fights who, as a sign of remorse, gave up their arms at the shrine, thereby renouncing violence and killing. This ritual is akin to making a vow.

All this is common knowledge in the Tibetan regions; those ordering military police raids on monasteries should know this full well. But those weapons left on the shrine as religious symbols came in handy for the authorities to incriminate Tibetan protesters, demonize monasteries and frame monks who never fire a gun as terrorists.

I recall in 2002, when Tenzin Delek Rinpoche of Garzê Tibetan Autonomous Prefecture in Sichuan Province was convicted of planning bombings, the authorities said a raid on his home had uncovered explosives, a secret chamber, and even lingerie. All this, the government said, was evidence of his terroristic bombings, covert activities and failure to observe Buddhist teachings. I had met the rinpoche before and was convinced he is a true believer who lives by his faith. While I could not believe these heinous accusations, I granted that the evidence was gathered following the protocol. So I set out for where he lived at the time of the raid, in Yajiang County in the southeastern part of the prefecture, and with the help of local Tibetans delved deeper into the circumstances.

Yajiang County is situated in a ravine with very little flat land. Any construction requires first carving into the steep hillside and manually leveling a piece of land—often with explosives. The rinpoche's house was only recently completed, so the explosives left over from its construction remained on the premises, as is the case in many local homes.

And the discovery of a secret chamber was more preposterous.

The house was built along an uneven hillside. The space between the rugged slope and the wall panels of the house was construed as a "secret compartment." As for the lingerie, the rinpoche's temple owns a commercial storefront, which was leased to a Han merchant to sell everyday items, including shorts and bras. When business slowed, the merchant shuttered his store. He turned in the unsold merchandise as rent-in-kind, and it was thrown in with the junk—and ultimately embellished as "evidence" of the rinpoche's promiscuity.

Truth be told, the authorities have long been embellishing evidence and framing the innocent. For instance, in 1958, before the Sixth Gungthang Rinpoche, Jigme Tenpe Wangchug, was accused of being the Amdo region's ringleader, police had planted hand grenades, a telegraph machine, etc. He was sentenced to twenty-one years in prison. Years later, a Tibetan police officer who had taken part in planting the evidence expressed his teary remorse toward his victim.

And in 1959, after the Dalai Lama and others went into exile, the Chinese Communist Party even made a show of "the crimes of the rebels." The evidence against the Dalai Lama's tutor Kyabje Trijang Rinpoche included a film projector, female mannequins, etc., all intended to demonstrate the monks' depravity.

All those items, in fact, belonged to the Lhasa elite colluding with the CCP.

* * *

The World's Youngest Political Prisoner

More than seventeen years ago, a six-year-old Tibetan boy vanished under mysterious circumstances. His disappearance captured the attention of the world, and he came to be known as the world's youngest political prisoner.

He is Gedhun Choekyi Nyima, confirmed by the Dalai Lama in accordance with Tibetan Buddhist tradition and rituals as the Eleventh

Panchen Lama, the second highest ranking monk in Tibetan Buddhism. On May 17, 1995, barely three days after he was named the incarnated successor to the Tenth Panchen Lama, he was spirited away by Chinese authorities from his home in the highlands of Lhari County in northern Tibet. He has since been permanently imprisoned in who knows where.

Through this time, organizations worldwide, including the United Nations Human Rights Council and its Committee on the Rights of the Child, have repeatedly demanded that the Chinese government release him and asked to visit him. Beijing has rebuffed these requests with all kinds of excuses.

Through this time, young Tibetan exiles and other young people around the world have protested his detention by displaying the eleven publicly available photos of Gedhun Choekyi Nyima. So far, he remains far away from his rightful home, the Tashilhunpo Monastery, and his family.

The only new development is that he is longer the world's youngest political prisoner. That dreadful distinction, ironically, has gone to yet another Tibetan. On September 30, 2006, Chinese border security fired on a group of Tibetan pilgrims on the Nangpa La pass near the Nepal-Tibet border, killing two youngsters and rounding up all those who did not manage to escape. Based on surveys with the survivors by international student organizations supporting Tibetan causes, as many as thirty pilgrims were likely "disappeared." Among those whose names and ages are known, there were at least a dozen minors; the youngest was only seven years old.

These underage detainees include: Tenwang, age 7; Lhakpa Tsering, 8; Dhondup Lhamo, 9; Dechen Dolma, 10; Wangchen, 11; Tsedon, 12; Sonam Wangdue, 12; Ming Shomo, 13; Lodoe Nyima, 15; Jamyang Tsetan, 16; Karma Tsetan, 16; and Lodoe Namkha, 16.

Whether all these children still remain behind bars, or have been banished to the streets as beggars and vagrants, or were bailed out by their parents, nobody knows. But for seventeen years, the title of the world's youngest political prisoner has gone to a Tibetan.

Time and again, China claims that its records on human rights are superior to those of most countries. But just how does Beijing justify locking up Tibetan children as young as six or seven years old?

* * *

Why Tibetans Flee to India?

When Chinese border patrol fired on a group of Tibetan pilgrims on the Nangpa La pass near the Nepal-Tibet border on September 30, 2006, there was shock and outcry worldwide, but then there was also disbelief. Many people wondered why the Tibetans must go to such lengths in order to sneak out of China. Why would they risk their lives, trek across the Himalayas and flee their homeland to India? If all they wanted was to make their pilgrimage, visit their family or study, why could they not go through the proper channel, apply for a passport and cross the border without perils?

Yes, these are the questions we Tibetans, too, want to have answered. But the answer rests not with the Tibetans, who have fled by the thousands, but with the Chinese government, whose practice has left Tibetans with no choice but exit the country in such an extraordinary manner.

In most of China, it is no longer difficult for citizens to travel outside its borders. All they need to do is go to the local public security bureau with an identification card, a photograph and two hundred yuan to apply for a passport, and it will be ready in a few days. Issuing passports is a sign of sovereignty of an independent country, and getting a passport is a citizen's basic entitlement. That has enabled a good number of Chinese to tour many countries, to trade, or to study.

However, except when they are sent overseas by the government, ordinary Tibetans find it rather difficult to go abroad. For Tibetans in Sichuan, Yunnan, Qinghai, and Gansu provinces, and especially in TAR, getting a passport is harder than going to space. They must go through the gauntlet of various levels of bureaucracy, reams of red tape and endless questioning. They sometimes even have to bribe officials with gifts and dinners. If they are lucky they get their passport within a year or so; more likely they will not get it at all. That is the case for both Tibetans who are employed in a work unit and those who are not. And it gets even more difficult for monks and nuns who don the cassocks.

Desperate circumstances call for desperate measures. Tibetans who want to make the pilgrimage, visit family or study must scale mountains and wade into rivers, brace for hunger and bitter cold, and endure blackmailing and other threats from crooks on the road, bleeding tens of thousands of yuan. Worse still, they also risk being arrested and locked up or even losing their lives. If they could get a passport as easily as other Chinese citizens, why would Tibetans go through this kind of trouble?

Not too long ago, it was easier for Tibetans from provinces outside TAR to get a passport. That was because they rode on the coattails of the Hans from these provinces to enjoy the same passport privileges.

Indeed, a few years ago when the Dalai Lama hosted a Kalachakra initiation ceremony in India, most of the nearly ten thousand Tibetans who made it hailed from these provinces. But on that occasion the Dalai Lama urged Tibetans to protect wildlife and to stop donning pelts. The Tibetans heeded his call by organizing large-scale pelt-burning activities in the Tibetan regions. After that, Beijing stopped issuing passports.

Since they cannot get a passport, Tibetans have to sneak out at all costs. Ultimately, it goes to show how Tibetans in China are denied the fundamental rights enjoyed by the majority of its citizens.

* * *

Helicopters over Stupas

A certain public security bureau chief in the Tibetan regions believes police helicopters are the most effective equipment to deploy to keep the peace. That is because only in a helicopter can officials rapidly traverse a sprawling, sparsely populated region to reach the crime scene. However, China does not have the know-how to manufacture helicopters that can operate on the Qinghai-Tibetan Plateau at 4,000 meters above sea level. Importing one costs nearly 10 million yuan, at least several times a Tibetan region's annual revenues—and that does not include the substantial operating and maintenance costs.

For years, Beijing has overlooked all these outlays by dismissing religion as a worthless enterprise and monks parasites. From the sociological perspective, if religion discourages people from committing crime, one can estimate how much society may save from such crime reduction. From this perspective alone, one cannot say religion is useless.

Whether it is against ecological sustainability or social stability, the most destructive element is human greed. Once people become greedy, they degenerate; once humankind becomes greedy, both Mother Nature and society are doomed to destruction. Stealing, robbing, poaching and destroying the environment—does greed not breed them all? No matter how draconian laws are, how powerful a police force is, and how expensive the helicopters it deploys, they are no match to greed.

China now boasts a few million police officers, and countless security guards and citizen soldiers in auxiliary forces, yet crime keeps growing, as does the budget on crime-fighting. If people do not dare commit crime only out of fear of police and the law, then does it not mean they surely will outside the reach of the rule of law?

No matter how many police officers there are, they will not outnumber the public and cannot possibly blanket places as sprawling as the Tibetan regions.

Religion does not require government subsidies or planning. All it needs is genuine freedom from government suppression; then religion will work its way to curb greed. As an investment it is the best bargain ever. On the contrary, Chinese authorities have mobilized massive resources to suppress Tibetan religion and launch "Help Tibet" campaigns to satisfy Tibetans' growing material needs. This will result in a vicious cycle: The sorrier the state religion is in, the stronger the greed, and the higher the crime rates.

It does not take long to build up a police force, but it takes much longer to build one's "internal police"—religious belief and a moral code of conduct. Once a people has lost its "internal police," it can take generations to recover.

* * *

Stampede in Jokhang

Established more than 1,300 years ago, the Jokhang Temple in Lhasa is the Tibetan regions' holiest. These days, it is deluged with tourists, mostly hailing from mainland China. In the summer months it averages 4,000 visitors a day. Taking into account worshippers from across the regions, the temple receives roughly 6,000 people day in day out.

In deference to worshippers, the temple bans tour groups of more than ten people between 8 a.m. and noon. The reality is the overwhelming volume of tourists has caused the ban to fall by the wayside, so worshippers and tourists are often cheek by jowl. The afternoon is reserved for tourists and no worshippers are allowed. After 6:30 p.m. it is time for class at the temple, so again worshippers and tourists are cheek by jowl. Annoyed, some worshippers wonder aloud: Is the temple built for the Buddhists or the tourists?

It is easy to see why anger has bubbled up. Worshipping Tibetans must stand in line to enter the temple, but tourists armed with admission tickets, following the lead of their flag-waving guide, can go straight in. "Please yield!" demand the tourists as they barge into the congregation of worshippers in prayer. Exasperated, some worshippers counter: "It's you who should yield. We're here to pray, so why should we make room for you?" Sensing the possibility for flare-ups, Tibetans would chide themselves for having almost lost it on temple ground.

But even the monks manning the admission booths would say, "So many tourists—that's upsetting. In the past, you smelled mostly the scent of burning incense and yak butter lamps; now it reeks only of stinky garlic."

Turns out the mastermind of this boom—the daughter of a Living Buddha who is now a high-level Chinese official—has been lining her own pocket. For each seventy-yuan ticket sold, she gets ten percent in commission. Assuming as many as 4,000 tickets are sold each day, can you imagine her daily take?

A few summers ago, monastery officials started handing out a pamphlet called "Dos and Don'ts While Visiting the Jokhang Temple." Among the pamphlet's seventeen guidelines are: Do not photograph or videotape monks and worshippers without their permission. Do not jostle or disturb worshippers in prayer. Observe the protocol and do not disrupt a Buddhist ceremony in progress. Obviously, these guidelines are aimed at the tourists' behavior. The shame is there is little effect on them; most do not abide by the guidelines.

Inside the temple, hordes of tourists listen to their own guides, mostly Chinese, all "politically correct" guides handpicked by the mainland's "Help Tibet" campaign; Tibetan guides become increasingly rare. These guides are most interested in elaborating on the thangkas, Tibetan embroidered silk paintings, and the jewelry that adorns the Buddha, with an eye to taking tourists to go shop for imitation items at the malls, where guides can expect kickbacks as much as forty to fifty percent.

The guides also dwell on politics, arguing that Tibet is part of China. Their favorite example is Princess Wencheng of Tang dynasty, whom they say brought this and that to Tibet. It is as though if it were not for her, Tibet would have no culture. To her credit, she did bring the sacred life-size statue of Gautama Buddha at age twelve. Slightly ahead of her was Nepal's Princess Bhrikuti Devi, who arrived with his sacred image at age eight. Both women were married to the King of Tubo (present-day Tibet), Songtsan Gambo, and both contributed to the spread of Buddhism in Tibet. But this alone cannot establish sovereignty over Tibet or the source of Tibetan culture.

Hearing the tour guides' propaganda, Tibetan worshippers trapped in the tourist crowd grumble, "Isn't it a distortion of Tibet's history?" But short of setting the record straight, they mostly keep their murmurs of discontent to themselves.

* * *

Barkor at Nightfall

One late night I passed by Sun Island, an isle in the Lhasa River, that local Tibetans have come to call Gumalingka, or Thieves' Island. Flooded with garish neon light, Sun Island served up a smorgasbord of vices for revelers to wine and dine, gamble and carouse. In a milieu full of din, dirt, and decadence, one did not feel like being in Tibet.

I headed over to the Barkor afterwards. There, in the shroud of respectful silence, the faint glimmers of streetlights and the lingering scent of incense, worshippers prayed and bowed as they circumambulated the Jokhang Temple. What a far cry from Sun Island.

Although I often am pessimistic about Tibet's current state of affairs, every time I set foot on the Barkor I feel otherwise, seeing the endless stream of circumambulating worshippers and the long line of the faithful prostrating before the likeness of Gautama Buddha. The gilded statues, the burning yak butter lamps, the crimson cassocks, and the symbols and jewelry donned by the worshippers—in all their glory and solemnity— seem to be part of an oil painting. That such a sacred pursuit still exists on earth is indeed touching.

A country mother poises her infant up close to the Buddha statue for blessings. A poor old man offers his only chipped coin smeared with dirt. A hunk of a grown man prostrates like a child. For them, this is not a ceremonial ritual but an ordinary routine deeply felt. Worshippers come in all shapes and forms—old and young, men and women, clerics and laypeople, city slickers and country folk, office workers and ordinary residents, in modern fashion or traditional garbs, in Nikes, leather shoes, or handcraft Tibetan boots. At Jokhang, they all are the faithful—bound by the belief that their destiny and their faith are intertwined. In other words, there is no difference among these worshippers. They are one and the same—the Tibetan people.

Although in the midst there are foreigners with a guidebook in hand, or gaggles of Chinese tourists led around by their guide, the worshippers have very little to do with others. Even though the tourists and the worshippers are at arm's length of each other, they are in two separate worlds. Oblivious of the tourists, Tibetans are in a world of their own, living and letting live.

How I wish all tourism could be like that: bringing in revenues without disrupting routines and destroying indigenous culture. To be sure, the reason why Jokhang's worshippers can sustain their culture in the thick of tourism all hinges on their religious faith. In a tourism economy without religion, locals and visitors would not be able to maintain their distance, and local culture would prove vulnerable in face of economic forces. That is why preserving Tibetan culture requires preserving Tibetan religion.

* * *

Highway Robbery in Holy Places

A friend who had toured Tibet during Saka Dawa[1] recounted a case of "robbery."

His tour group of thirty-some people were herded to a monastery in the heart of Lhasa said to be a Buddhist academy. They were immediately impressed: The shrine had aged well. Buddha statues stirred one's awe amidst the swirling incense smoke and the chanting lamas.

Then, the group was introduced to the Living Buddha for consecration; everyone was touched. At that critical moment, however, the group was told the Living Buddha could not deliver his predictions in Mandarin. It so happened a Mandarin-speaking eminent monk was on hand to offer his predictions.

The "eminent monk" chose to meet with the tour group members one by one. In fluent Mandarin, he recited clichés commonly employed by shamans and charlatans in mainland China. For instance, he would say so and so has got a broad forehead and an auspicious appearance that promises prosperity. But then in the next breath this "eminent monk" would warn the fortune seekers that they might soon run into bad luck and suffer in the hands of foes. To upend this doom, the only way is to burn strong incense with sincerity.

---

1.   Saka Dawa is a sacred period commemorating Lord Buddha's birthday.

My friend did not understand, so he kept asking how he could show sincerity. Said the eminent monk: "Sincerity is determined by the amount of money." Just how much is sincere enough? Three thousand yuan at least, or even thirty thousand—the more the better.

My friend tried to talk his way out, saying that he was traveling without so much cash.

"No problem," the eminent monk said, "we take credit cards here."

By then it dawned on my friend the holy façade was a scam: It was all about money. His deference dissolved into disgust, and he wanted to walk out. But it would seem too drastic, as he was alone with the monk. In the end, my friend got out three hundred yuan poorer. When the members regrouped, they all said they had been forced to pay, with my friend losing the least money. Some were set back by as much as a few thousand yuan. They were convinced that the one-on-one was a set up and felt robbed.

And that was not it. Along the way the tour group encountered three more of such scams, including one at Qinghai's Kumbum Monastery (Ta'er in Chinese). Their experiences in Tibet were a huge letdown.

———

When my friend sent me pictures of the monastery where he was "robbed," I forwarded them to friends in Lhasa for identification. I was both shocked and ashamed to learn it was Gyumé Dra-tsang, the famous academy of the Gelug sect of Buddhism. So on a recent trip to Lhasa, I made it a point to go there and investigate.

Once there, I told the few young monks I ran into what had happened to my friend and that many people had thought it all was the monks' doing, thus hurting the reputation of the monastery as well as Tibetan Buddhism.

"How would the monks do something like that?" I asked. In a rare show of rage, the young monks told me the story.

What happened was earlier in the year a tour company called Guilin International—armed with an edict from Lhasa's religion and tourism bureaux—approached the monastery. In order to publicize its significance in Buddhism and boost its revenues, the monastery was asked to sign an agreement with the tour company for it to set up gift shops to sell paraphernalia, and to arrange for interpreters because the monks do not speak Mandarin or English. The monastery had no choice but cooperate.

The tour company's dozen employees stationed themselves at the temple as staff members. A few young women assumed the role of docents but identified themselves to tourists as "volunteers."

Four of the male employees had shaved their heads and donned cassocks. They presented themselves as Buddhist students brought in by the monastery or the "Help Tibet" monks dispatched from mainland China. Some even pretended to be Mandarin-speaking Tibetan assistants arranged by the tourism bureau to interpret for the "Living Buddha," an old monk who chanted for tourists. They set up shop all over the monastery and met with tourists in private, claiming to perform various rites for them, such as sprinkling consecration, opening one's eyes, praying for a good future, and obtaining the Buddha's power—for a gratuity, the higher the better.

The tour company also set up a chain of four stores to sell sacred items. A pack of yak butter (for lighting lamps) priced at eight yuan at one of the stores on the Barkor was once sold for 3,900 yuan by the tour company, after the staff wrapped it in a *khata*, a ceremonial silk scarf, and dressed it up as the holiest offering.

The monks could not bear to watch the con games, so they took the initiative to warn unsuspecting tourists. But the tourists did not believe the monks, perhaps because of their halting Mandarin. When some of the monks got into an argument with the docents over their perfunctory talks, they even threatened to call the police.

When the monks took their complaints to the religion bureau they invariably fell on deaf ears. "The tour company has got officials' backing so it doesn't matter how many complaints we file," one of the monks told me.

Finally, when a Taiwanese tour group lodged a complaint about being cheated, the officials had to act. The tour company's employees decamped from the monastery.

The religion bureau has hardly cleaned house. In Lhasa, reportedly there still are seven or eight such bureaucrat-backed tour companies, probably running the same or similar scams inside other temples. That means countless tourists are bound to run into scams as my friend did.

Besides the tourists, the biggest losers are Tibet and Tibetan Buddhism.

Chapter IV
Wrecking Nature

Siphoning off Tibetan Water

My friends in Tibet are anguished about the damming activities all over Kham (Qinghai and Gansu provinces) because nearly every waterway has been taken over. The major rivers are being developed by powerful conglomerates; minor tributaries are divided up among local bosses. Colluding with municipal officials, these developers are seizing watersheds in near mania.

These days, damming, land expropriation, and relocation are widespread in Kham. Almost every county has set up its own "migration bureau," whose real mandate is to evict people from their ancestral land. Every single project goes under the banner of national necessities. It seems what the nation needs is beyond question. Who cares what Tibetans need and what Tibetans think?

Tibetans are most worried about the western route of the South-North Water Transfer project:[1] One proposal on the table calls for channeling water from the Yalong, the Tongtian, and the Dadu, all tributaries of the Yangtze in the southwest, to the upper Yellow River. My friends were shocked when I mentioned another plan, proposed by a hydrologist, connecting the Yarlung Tsangpo in western Tibet through a canal to Tianjin, a city seventy miles southeast of Beijing. This will channel as much as two hundred billion cubic meters of water—equivalent to four

---

1. The feasibility of this route is still being studied and it remains unclear when, or if, the project will begin, but construction work for the other two routes—central and eastern—is underway.

times the Yellow River's annual flow—from Tibet to the parched Chinese mainland.

Beijing unveiled the plans to much fanfare, proclaiming that simulations of the western route would be based on high-resolution topographical data fed into supercomputers. Although the simulations had yet to be done and results remained uncertain, supporters of the plans were already extremely gung-ho. They said the western-route project would be one for the nation's history book for the current leaders, whetting their appetite for grand gestures and edifices. However, even if mega-dams and super-long canals pipe water of the Yarlung Tsangpo into the Yellow River, can they mitigate all the problems created by the water transfer?

It is already a consensus among scientists that human activities have caused climate change. So would the water transfer, a human undertaking on a massive scale, not further climate change? Advocates for the western route justified the project by saying it was global warming that had caused water shortage. Would redistributing water and upsetting the balance of Mother Nature not exacerbate global warming and water shortage? All these repercussions are far beyond computer modeling.

A Tibetan environmentalist based in the Yangtze source region shared his concerns with much sadness: For Tibetans, climate change once was farthest from their minds, but now it is a matter of life and death. Tibetans are bearing the brunt of human activity-induced climate change. The ever-shrinking Arctic and Antarctica, after all, are sparsely inhabited, but the ecologically fragile Qinghai-Tibetan Plateau is the Tibetans' only home.

* * *

Herders Are Strangers on Their Land

When the Three Rivers National Nature Reserve was established in the area boasting the sources of the Yangtze, the Yellow River and the Mekong, local Tibetan herders were being resettled in the City of Golmud (Ge'ermu in Chinese). In the beginning, the relocated herders were elated because they had long aspired to urban life. Now that the government was building them houses and giving them a stipend, it simply could not be better. So they pulled up stakes on the grassland and headed for the city.

To keep up with city folks, herders moving into a new house need to buy a full suite of new furniture, but they can hardly afford it. With the influx of herders the prices of used furnishing have shot up. Before, four hundred yuan could buy a full suite; now even a table costs just as much.

Some people liken the herders entering the market to kids in the candy store: They want anything and everything. They are buying cars and TVs, and learning to use mobile phones. And they put on make-up, eat out and go to clubs. In short order they use up all their money. They learn to spend money as city folks do but cannot make a living the same way. They have come to live by the rules of the market but are unable to get ahead under such rules. Without a livelihood, they linger on the streets, window shopping and watching how city folks spend their money. These erstwhile herders feel the pinch more than ever, but how can they make a quick buck?

On the Qinghai-Tibet highway between Golmud and Lhasa, a new type of crime has appeared in recent years. The suspect would lie in wait along the highway and lasso a passing motorcycle. After throwing the cyclist off his vehicle, the suspect would take off on it. Judging from the *modus operandi*, one cannot help but guess only the herders possess the skills to pull off such a crime.

The impact of relocation on the herders is not confined to the city; the repercussions have spilled over to their villages and their tribes. In fact, the herders' recent experiences have shown the market economy is like a wolf charging into their herd. Defenseless against the onslaught, the herders are being chased around instead.

Once the euphoria of moving into the city subsides, reality sets in: The herders realize that they have left behind not only the grassland but also their livelihood. They sink to the bottom rung of society. In the city, they find only gigs like digging ditches. The awkward way these herders wield the spades is just like how their elders toiled half a century ago, when they were sent down to labor camps, some older Tibetans recall painfully. Like their elders, the herders are doing the same work, and they, too, have left the grasslands for the sandy-pebbled Gobi Desert.

However much it seems the herders have left of their own volition, in this day and age in Tibet, volition is at best a kind of delusion.

* * *

Every Inch of Land Is Sacred

In Tibetan environmentalist Rinchen Samdrup's hometown, Tserangding in Gonjo County (Gongjue in Chinese), Chamdo Prefecture of TAR, there is a sacred mountain called Senggenamzong.

During his grandfather's time, Samdrup[2] recalls, Senggenamzong was covered with dense forests, home to tigers and untamed tribal men. Later, all the trees were chopped down, denuding the mountain.

In 2003, Samdrup led 1,300 fellow villagers in setting up an NGO called Voluntary Environmental Protection Association of Kham Anchung Senggenamzong. Together, they began to plant trees on the bald hillside. And following the tradition, village households took turns in sending family members to patrol the hillside on horseback, guarding against poaching and illegal logging.

The villagers also set about cleaning up the mountain. In the beginning, villagers would burn or bury the garbage they picked up, but soon they realized this would cause more pollution. The garbage was left behind mostly from digging for caterpillar fungi, a livelihood for most locals.

So instead of banning the digging, the villagers asked the fungus diggers to pick up after themselves, fill in the pits, and replenish the turf.

---

2.   Samdrup was sentenced to five years in prison in 2010 allegedly for showing sympathies for the Dalai Lama.

Because if they do not, the pasture would be destroyed in three years and there would be no more fungi. All this is for sustainable development.

Samdrup also started an annual journal, in Tibetan, called *Self-Awareness*, giving full play to both national environmental regulations and Buddhist teachings on ecological protection. In the journal, Samdrup explained the Tibetan belief in sacredness of landscape is no superstition—but a culture of environmental protection that has evolved historically.

Thanks to the ecological fragility of the Tibetan Plateau, its inhabitants have deeply felt experiences of disasters. Such experiences not only inform their culture, religion and customs, but also shape their ecological view. In Tibetans' eyes, all living beings are created equal and should be respected as such. That is how Tibetans have lived in harmony with nature.

In other parts of China, environmental protection is being done either out of the necessity to clean up industrial waste or under duress of the law and economic interest, Samdrup observed, rather than out of respect for other living beings. "But for our villagers, to protect the environment is to abide by our traditional culture," Samdrup said, "which we are all too happy to do even if for no other reasons."

Some environmental experts say ethnic groups protect the natural environment proactively mostly out of their reverence for sacred mountains and lakes. China has established many nature reserves, only to find both staff and funding stretched too thin. Often a single official is put in charge of ten thousand square kilometers, rendering effective management all but impossible. It behooves conservation officials to tap into grassroots efforts.

Samdrup said he lives by these words of the world-renowned American conservationist and naturalist, George Schaller: "Every inch of the planet needs protection. Every inch of our land is sacred."

* * *

Betting on Tibetan Land

There is a popular saying among mine owners in Tibet: "Make a killing by day, ride home before nightfall." That means anyone who stumbles upon a good mine will haul in buckets and buckets of gold, instantly. This kind of get-rich-quick scheme is reminiscent of the dot-com boom of the 1990s. Returns on investments are at least a hundred times.

Most mine prospectors in Tibet have a gambler's mentality. They all dream of making their seed money back many times over, though very few have realized overnight riches. Mining in Tibet is very much like gambling: Chances that bettors would lose are rather high.

That is because geological survey data in Tibet are very imprecise. With most mines, no one can tell how much ore there is, how good it is, how to get it—or if there is even any to begin with. I have once heard of a prospector buying up an entire hill in Lhasa, plunking down more than half a million yuan. But the few dozen tons of lead-zinc ore he was able to dig up was worth just one percent of his investment.

If the same amount of money were put into real estate, even when one is stuck holding the land at least there would be a house somewhere. With mine prospecting, failures leave one empty-handed.

However, some prospectors did manage to reap a bounty, precisely because of the imprecise geological data. The TAR Mining Bureau is charged with issuing permits for excavations, theoretically speaking. But since the bureau's officials are clueless about what lies beneath their feet, they have become more or less toothless overseers.

These days, most prospectors do not even bother to go through the mining bureau; instead they deal directly with local officials. Because the officials also have no idea of what a mine might yield, they generally do not charge prospectors high fees. This leaves plenty of room for handsome profits.

Despite the dearth of data, few prospectors would bother with any survey before digging. Doing a survey entails onerous procedures and costs at least several million yuan, leaving prospectors with little money to spend on excavations. So they forge ahead and drill—and drill. Much like blind cats chasing mice, the miners randomly blast drill holes all over a hill, and they keep at it until they unearth a deposit.

They count themselves lucky if they strike ore after spending only hundreds of thousands of yuan on drilling. Many prospectors have had to abandon their mines after squandering millions and still coming up empty.

These prospectors have turned the Tibetan landscape into one big casino. At issue is not just the desecration of Mother Nature, but also the destruction of mineral resources. Thorough surveying and responsible mining would help keep the land in a better shape and increase yield and efficiency, whereas these gambler-miners cherry-pick from mines and lay waste quality ores.

Where mine prospectors pursue profits, Tibetans pay the price.

* * *

How Fur Becomes Tibetan Fashion

Not too long ago at a Kalachakra initiation ceremony in Guntur, India, the Dalai Lama criticized the growing trend of China's Tibetans donning animal skins. The fact is, once upon a time, except for the Khampa elite in eastern Tibet who adorned their collars, cuffs and lapels with small strips of fur, few Tibetans wore anything other than cloth, silk, traditional woolen fabric, or lambskin harvested from their own herd.

Yet, today, when protecting wildlife is the badge of civilization and the anti-fur movement is all the rage worldwide, ever more Tibetans see wearing animal skins as being trendy. The furs of all kinds of rare animals, such as foxes, otters, leopards and even tigers, are in. And they appear in ever larger strips.

When Sonam Wangmo, Tibetan pop sensation and gold medalist at a nationwide young-singers' contest, performed on TV recently, her costume was made mostly of fur. It made one wonder what had happened to the wild animals.

Fur serves one's vanity and little else. It does not make for the most practical of apparel. When Tibetans deck out in their minks during the Tibetan New Year and break a sweat under the blazing Lhasa sun, they look so ridiculous.

The Dalai Lama's censure aside, here is a question we should ponder: How come Tibetans pursue fashion trends that go against the times? I believe that may have everything to do with the "culture-based" economic development campaign launched by officials in the Tibetan regions. In order to promote tourism and attract investments, these officials have spearheaded a raft of "cultural festivals," in which the signature event is a traditional-costume show.

Official aesthetics rule the day. Models donning expensive costumes and accessories often get the nod. This naturally encourages everyone to put on the rarest and largest pieces of pelts. Sometimes the officials would even borrow jewelry from the public and pile it on the models, turning them into flesh-and-blood showcases—gaudy to the extreme. The officials also dispatch policemen to be the models' bodyguards and make sure the jewelry will not be lost or stolen.

Such shows invariably attract media coverage. As images of these decked-out models become prevalent, more Tibetans try to emulate. A pop star like Wangmo is not only a trendsetter for Tibetan youths, but for outsiders also a Tibetan icon. Those who learn about Tibetan culture solely through the media would think all Tibetans don animal skins and must have been slaughtering wild animals since time immemorial.

This cannot be further from the truth. Tibetans show compassion for all living beings and avoid killing at all costs. There is a lesson to be learned from this distortion: Exploiting culture only for economic gains will ultimately create an ugly culture.

* * *

Disappearing Lhasa

In 1996, several architects from Germany, Portugal, and other countries founded the Tibet Heritage Fund in Lhasa. Its goal was "to provide a better understanding of the fabric of Lhasa and of the Tibetan traditional architecture and so to contribute to their preservation and adequate development."

However, what they soon found was "an average of 35 buildings per year have been torn down since 1993, except in 1999 and 2000."[3]

And by 2001, two Norway-based architects Knud Larsen and Amund Sinding-Larsen, aided by many local experts and scholars, concluded after their seven-year-long survey of Lhasa that "[i]n the mid-1980s, most religious and secular buildings remained intact, but today [in 2001] the number of such standing structures has been reduced by more than a third, to approximately 200. With limited open land for expansion, the future safeguarding of Lhasa's historical core has become critical. And yet there is a growing recognition, very late in the day, of the importance of this cultural heritage."[4]

Their findings resulted in a book called *The Lhasa Atlas: Traditional Tibetan Architecture and Townscape*, which appeared in Chinese and Tibetan in 2005.

In deference to tradition, no one in Lhasa was allowed to build anything taller than, or even as tall as, the Potala Palace. In 1994, the palace became a UNESCO World Heritage site. With this recognition came stringent restrictions on surrounding construction. Even so, offending high-rises have sprung up around the palace.

Similarly, in adherence to tradition, no structure around the Jokhang Temple also should tower over it. And, by 2000, the temple, as well as the surrounding Barkor, made the list of heritage sites. Yet, little did that stop newly-built hotels and shopping malls from overshadowing the temple.

---

3.   Both quotations are from Tibet Heritage Fund's website: http://www.tibet heritagefund.org/old_web/menu_main/2_fs_en.html, accessed September 2, 2013.

4.   *The Lhasa Atlas: Traditional Tibetan Architecture and Townscape* (Chicago: Serindia Publications, 2001), 18.

By 2007, historic sites in the old city of Lhasa, including the Potala, were so endangered by surrounding development that UNESCO issued a "yellow card," warning that they risked being stripped of the heritage recognition.

The ugliest structure in all of Lhasa, no doubt, is the Tibet Liberation Memorial Monument. Despite criticisms from UNESCO and other international organizations, the monument went up on the square facing the Potala Palace. Billed as an abstract representation of Mt. Everest, the memorial looks more like a crude missile. Devoid of any aesthetic value, it acts like a spear that pierces Tibetans' hearts.

A close contender in the ugliest architecture contest is the information technology building of the Tibet Public Security Bureau. The building, a "Help Tibet" campaign gift from the prosperous Jiangsu Province, was inserted between Jokhang and Sera monasteries, blocking the direct view from the Jokhang's top floor. Over objections from UNESCO and other global bodies, the building opened in 2002 and became the height-limit-flouting poster child.

The demolition of traditional architecture mars not only the heritage but also the symbols of Tibetan culture. In the name of modernization, de facto colonization has advanced further. What have been disappearing are not just old buildings but also the Tibetans' way of life along with them. The ubiquitous ugly new buildings have despoiled Tibet's unique, age-old cultural and natural outlook. And their impact on the region's ecology and environment is irreparable, and even unforgivable.

* * *

Regret in a Half-Century

Lhasa is changing.

The city center keeps expanding, the streets keep widening, and the buildings keep soaring. Jumbotrons crop up everywhere on thorough-fares and neon lights flood the sidewalks. An underground walkway

Figure 9

The authorities' appetite for resources has proved voracious. They mine for ores wherever there are hills, and dam wherever there are rivers for power—all in the name of development.

Figure 10

The pristine landscape is pockmarked with mines, both active and aborted.

Figure 11

An old Lhasa temple destroyed during the Cultural Revolution lies waste. A mall rises a stone's throw away.

Figure 12

Remnants are turned into a tourist attraction.

Figure 13

A bulldozer in the Potala. Under the banner of modernization, Old Lhasa is being demolished.

Figure 14

An exiled nun lingers in the ruins.

Figure 15

Forced to relocate, herders pick up stakes and head for the city.

Figure 16

Resettled into villages replete with modern amenities, herders are cut off from their indigenous livelihoods.

Figure 17

All decked out à la official aesthetics. This is how fur becomes Tibetan fashion.

is now connected to the Potala Palace plaza, where streetlights flare throughout the night, loudspeakers blare, and musical fountains spray.

In Old Lhasa, demolition is what all residents talk about. The masses have abandoned their traditional homes for modern apartments that are sprouting like wild flowers. The New Lhasa on the government's drawing board is one enormous sprawl, annexing a county dozens of miles away to be connected with a tunnel.

To be sure, many locals welcome the change, as well as the prosperity, convenience, and comfort that come with it. That way, they feel they can enjoy the same good life in Lhasa as in the mainland. Local Tibetans should be the judge and there is no place for outsiders to pontificate, lest they be seen as monopolizing the benefits of modernization and condemning others as objects of curiosity in ethnic backwaters.

No doubt Tibetans should have every right to enjoy modernization. I just hope they would take the long view and consider the lessons learned by the Chinese, who have gone down the same path.

Recalling the Beijing of yesteryears: When the old city wall and moat still stood, in their embrace were the palaces and royal residences, the courtyard houses and *hutongs*—all in beautiful complete harmony with the surroundings.

Then the CCP rose to power. Under the banner of modernization and the call by Mao Zedong to prioritize the new at the expense of the old, the bulldozer came rolling in and there went most of the capital's relics. Today, Beijing is chockfull of cars, overpasses, and high-rises. The city has become much richer, yet poorer in cultural characteristics.

Old Peking versus New Beijing—which is better? Voicing her objection over dismantling the capital's 500-year-old city wall, famous architect Lin Huiyin[5] once said, "In fifty years, you will regret it."

---

5.   Lin Huiyin 林徽因, known as Phyllis Lin in the West, was modern China's first female architect. She studied architecture at the University of Pennsylvania under Paul Cret. Her niece is the renowned Chinese-American architect and sculptor Maya Lin, who designed the Vietnam Veterans Memorial.

As a half-century has just gone by, sure enough it is too late for Beijing to regret it.

Every city is a cultural whole unto itself. Simply preserving a few scenic spots piecemeal does not serve to retain a city's historical heritage. These days, when regarding Lhasa from a vantage point, one is hard put to find fluttering prayer flags and wafting incense smoke. Instead, bland standard-issue cement rooftops fill the skyline, and several ugly buildings have risen to become Lhasa's new landmarks.

Now, whenever I look around I hear echoes of Lin's prophetic words: "In fifty years, you will regret it."

Chapter V
Culture Twisted, Trampled

Scrapping Tibetan Lessons for Stability

I still remember, on October 19, 2010, thousands of middle and high school students in Regong of Amdo raised small blackboards with their demand chalked in Tibetan: "We need Tibetan classes." This demonstration to defend their mother tongue was soon joined by countless schoolchildren across Amdo and Tibetan regions in Qinghai and Gansu provinces. Even many Tibetan students at Beijing's Central University for Nationalities made the same appeal.

I still remember more than three hundred Tibetan teachers sent a joint letter to Qinghai's provincial committee demanding that Tibetan students be primarily taught in their mother tongue. The teachers opposed the "mostly Chinese, supplemented with Tibetan" curriculum and its expansion into kindergarten. Retired cadres and veteran educators in Tibet also submitted opinions to the education and united front ministries in support of this demand.

Still I remember the party secretary of Qinghai later recommended that bilingual education reforms be strategically and gradually adopted. His words certainly aimed to appease. Innocent Tibetans trusted that officials would keep their word and never thought that was merely a stalling tactic.

In less than one-and-a-half year, the other shoe dropped. In March 2012, fresh into the new semester, schoolchildren in Tibetan and ethnic schools in Qinghai and Gansu provinces discovered that suddenly Tibetan learning materials had been replaced with Chinese-language textbooks. In other words, the rug of bilingual education had been pulled from under Tibetan students. Just imagine what impact it had on children of Tibetan farmers and herdsmen.

On March 3, 2012, Tsering Kyi, a ninth-grader from Machu in Amdo set herself on fire in protest. And on March 14, thousands of students from high schools and teachers' colleges across Amdo took to the streets to voice their demands for linguistic equality, national equality, and local autonomy.

The reason why Tibetan education has landed on the chopping block time and again is more than cultural—it is political, as evidenced by a document outlining education reforms in Qinghai Province. Implementing Chinese-language education is deemed "a major political task" in the Tibetan regions. So concluded the officials in the wake of the 2008 riots: To exterminate Tibetan-language education will be crucial to maintaining harmony and political stability.

"Maintaining stability is as much about keeping the political situation calm as about winning over the hearts and minds of the public," a teacher from Amdo reasoned on-line. "If we cannot even win over the hearts and minds of our children, just how can we maintain stability in the Tibetan regions?"

Centuries ago, the Spanish *conquistadores* occupied the Mayan land and wiped the Mayan language off the face of the earth. Decades ago, the Cultural Revolution sought to eradicate Tibetan-language teaching so that a whole generation of Tibetans like me lost our native language.

This time, though, will be quite different. As nineteen-year-old Kyi who died from self-immolation has shown, lives in defense of the Tibetan tongue will not be extinguished.

* * *

Must Children Trade Roots for Books?

A Chinese friend of mine, who is passionate about Tibetan culture, went to Kham to start a school. After toughing it out for the better part of a year, she found it hard to keep running the school under the most trying of circumstances. So she now tries a different tack: She would handpick a dozen children, take them out of the country to the urban Karze (Ganzi in Chinese) region in eastern Tibet and send them to school there at her expense and on the donations she has raised.

While I respect her, I question her method. So I asked her for what she educates these children. If she hopes to educate the children so they will serve their people and their land, then sending them off to the city will not accomplish this goal. Once educated in the city, the children would try to stay at all costs, turning their back on their village. Even when they go back, they would miss the city and leave again the first chance they get. That is because the baptism of urban education will turn them into something quite different from their elders in the country. As soon as my friend takes the children to the city she also plucks their roots.

To be sure, education may not be all about serving the people; it can serve only the children's interest. True that they get the chance to leave behind the hardscrabble life on the grassland and become urbanites. If that is the intent, here is the risk: Will the children be accepted in the city? If they are, then it is all well and good. But if they are not, then they will live in limbo and suffer a lifetime of anguish and problems. In that case, not only would the village lose its children, but the children also would lose their happiness.

Many herders and farmers are unwilling to send their children off to school. One cannot chalk it up as mere ignorance and backwardness. If after graduation their children can find work in the city and are fully embraced as city folks, most parents would be most willing to let them go. But the reality is they cannot find work in the city. And they come back to their village and know nothing about farming or herding. Boys become never-do-wells and girls know only grooming. They do not even know to look under to find the udders, so goes a common country saying.

So I told my friend: When she goes to the Tibetan regions to work in education, she should not assume Hans are the only keepers of civilization and she is there to tame the natives and change their way of living. Tibetan locals' way of life follows from their path of civilization. Their civilization differs from the Hans' only in trajectory, not in quality. What she considers best for the Tibetan children might not be something they can enjoy, or even attain. To impose on them what she thinks is best may work against what she intends.

The kind of education they need should be rooted in their folkways and indigenous livelihood—but not one that supplants their civilization with others'.

* * *

Ye All Celebrate Chinese Festivals

In late 2007, China's premier announced certain traditional Chinese festivals, namely, Tomb Sweeping, Dragon Boat, and Mid-Autumn festivals, be made national holidays. In a country that boasts 1.3 billion people and fifty-six ethnic groups, everyone must now celebrate these three Han festivals.

The diktat was a long time coming, in the wake of much deliberation and dissent. The resurrection of these traditional festivals, amid mounting nationalism, was affirmed by pro-government scholars as a shot in the arm for national unity and a boost to the country's cultural soft power. China Central TV aired a series called *Our Festivals*, complementing an official publication of the same title. But all it featured were Han festivals, none of other ethnic groups.

An article in the *People's Daily*, the government's mouthpiece, called these traditional festivals the most outstanding manifestation of Chinese culture, touting the move to make the festivals national holidays as an increasingly clear expression of Chineseness. These festivals would be important signs of cultural and national recognition for the people in China.

For Hans, Tomb Sweeping, Dragon Boat, and Mid-Autumn are traditional red-lettered days for the Hans, each hailing from a legend and corresponding with different seasons. Tomb Sweeping Festival is related to Han burial rituals. Dragon Boat Festival commemorates a revered figure of an ancient era. Mid-Autumn is a time for family reunions. All this is part of Hans' cultural tradition—but of no other ethnic groups in China. It is all well and good for Hans to celebrate their festivals. The Mid-Autumn practice of gifting and eating mooncakes traces its origin to the waning years of Yuan dynasty, when the Hans were plotting to overthrow the Mongol rule. Legend has it that Han rebels communicated with each other by slipping their message into the mooncakes: "Slaughter the Mongols by Mid-Autumn." Be it fact or legend, many Mongols in China take offence at this festival. Mandating its celebration nationwide clearly shows Beijing's Han-centric mentality.

As for Tibetans, few know what these festivals are about. But since they are made national holidays, it means Tibetans, especially the children, are being gradually homogenized during festive celebrations.

Just as the *People's Daily* article predicts, "After a number of years, our children will get used to hiking to visit their ancestors' tomb site during Tomb Sweeping Festival and admiring the full moon during Mid-Autumn. Who can say this is not thanks to the influence of these festivals, which allow them to understand the meaningful manifestation of cultural China?"

This reminds me of my school years,[1] when I could fluently recite Tang- and Song-dynasty poems but was totally ignorant of any work by Jetsun Milarepa, one of Tibet's most famous poets. I could go on and on about the construction of the Great Wall under the reign of the First Emperor, yet I could not begin to explain how the Potala was built. My knowledge about Lu Xun, the renowned Chinese novelist, far exceeded what I knew about the Sixth Dalai Lama, Tsangyang Gyatso. In fact, over a long, long time the manifestation of my identity has evolved. I have taught myself everything I know about my people—because in my heart of hearts I see Tibet as my land.

Without a doubt, Tomb Sweeping, Dragon Boat, and Mid-Autumn festivals are Han manifestations. However, Beijing chose to mandate such manifestations, meaning other ethnic groups had no choice but

---

1.   Woeser was born to Tibetan parents in Lhasa but raised in Sichuan Province.

recognize them. In other words, in a harmonized China, manifestations of other ethnic cultures are bound to be supplanted, or eliminated.

* * *

Official Ban a Helpful Reminder

Perhaps we should thank our authoritarian government for its devious way to publicize Tibetan tradition and history. Thanks to Beijing's efforts to snuff out our cultural practices, ever more Tibetans, especially the younger generation, are taking them to heart.

Recently, Beijing has come down with a ban on Lhabab Düchen, one of Tibet's many traditional festivals, commemorating the descent of Buddha from heaven.

This, ironically, has reminded many Tibetans of this red-lettered day. Truth be told, today as the Western calendar is prevailing and the Tibetan calendar is phasing out of daily life, many busy people have become oblivious of the spiritual significance and ancient traditions passed down through the festivals. Not just the dates but even the names have slipped their mind.

Thanks to the ham-handed bans, we instead are alerted to the festivals. The "alert" typically works like this: Angered by a meeting at work, a Tibetan would say, "Here it goes another meeting, here it goes again they tell us not to attend a certain ceremony tomorrow, or we'll be punished . . ." Then the listeners would inquire what is on tomorrow. Tomorrow may be Monlam Chenmo, the Great Prayer Festival that falls in the first Tibetan calendar month; or Saka Dawa, celebrating the birth and enlightenment of Buddha and his entry to nirvana on the fifteenth day of the fourth Tibetan calendar month; or Incense Festival; or the Dalai Lama's birthday, on July 6; or Drukpa Tse-Shar, also known as Dharma Wheel Festival, on the fourth day of the sixth Tibetan calendar month; or the twenty-fifth day of the tenth Tibetan calendar month, when the death of Tsong Khapa, who founded the Geluk school of Tibetan Buddhism, is commemorated with lamps and bonfires atop monasteries. Naturally, what has begun as a rant would gradually deepen into a discussion of the festivals' origins, rituals, and meaning. For some, it is a trip down memory lane; for others, it can be an enlightening lecture. Both speakers and listeners pay full attention, and few will ever forget these festivals again.

Sadly, though, certain festivals have been vulgarized. For example, Shoton Festival, also known as Yogurt Festival, falls on the first day of the seventh month of the Tibetan calendar. It is a festival that traces its origins to pilgrims coming to serve monks with yogurt, but now becomes a day merchants capitalize on to make a quick buck. And on the fifteenth day of the tenth month, which commemorates Palden Lhamo, the only female deity among the traditional "Eight Guardians of the Law," the festival now turns into a time when women ask men for handouts. But there are those who recall their roots and cherish their cultural traditions.

In addition, there are certain politically sensitive months, such as March, September and December, when the entire city of Lhasa is in a near-lockdown and restrictions are the order of the day. For example, the anniversary of the Tibetan Uprising Day on March 10, 1959. Mass protests broke out in September 1987 and March 1989. December 10, 1989 was the day the Dalai Lama was honored with the Nobel Peace Prize. All these have helped remind many Tibetans, especially the younger generation, of the important events that mark the regions' turbulent past half-century. By taking these anniversaries to heart, Tibetans can trace the trail of blood and tears: the defeat and sacrifice, resilience and honor, shared by six million souls.

For all that, we must thank a regime that seeks to shackle Tibetans' hearts and minds. Time after time it hands down unconstitutional bans that serve only to strengthen the traditions, restore the traumatized memories, and boost the awareness and pride of generation after generation of Tibetans.

Eternally grateful!

* * *

Ringing in the Tibetan New Year

Not too long ago I received a text message so meaningful that it is worth being put on paper. "Let's act: Toss out Lunar New Year and bring back Tibetan New Year," it says. "Our one small step will speak volumes to our offspring in the snow country."

This text message reminds me of the many new years I spent in Kham of eastern Tibet. All I recall are Lunar New Year's celebrations and none of Tibetan New Year. Tibetans all around us seem to have taken it for granted. From Lunar New Year's eve on for two weeks long they set off firecrackers, have reunion dinners, collect red packets, visit each other, and take turns hosting banquets. That is not how Tibetan New Year is celebrated.

This text message also reminds me that in 2006 on my blog on www. Tibetcul.com—before it was shut down by the authorities—I suggested that we Tibetans had been ringing in the New Year at the wrong time because for ages we had based it on the Lunar calendar. This garnered a lot of comments, and the consensus was it was time to synchronize New Year's celebrations with our calendar.

In fact, under the lead of enlightened Tibetans this is effectively underway in certain areas. For example, in the Tibetan regions in Qinghai and Sichuan provinces the Tibetan New Year is now a public holiday and locals have revived their celebrations based on the Tibetan calendar. However, the forces of sinicization remain unrelenting and the force of habit takes time to overcome, many Tibetans still celebrate the Chinese Spring Festival as their new year. Thus, the text message I received serves as a meaningful reminder, though some might dismiss its significance. This is not just about righting an out-of-sync festival but affirming a people's identity.

For most in the modern world, traditional festive celebrations serve more symbolic than practical purposes. But for the colonized—those who suffer exploitation, conversion, and homogenization—these details matter. The New Year's celebrations is an obvious example. For us Tibetans across the regions, celebrating our traditional festivals is an affirmation and expression of our ethnic identity. This is not something that can be supplanted.

Although we live in the age of globalization, we should not turn ourselves into Hans or other peoples. To claim our place in the world, fight for our rights, make our voices heard, and show our true colors, we must remain rooted in the soil of our cultural tradition and insist that it not be swallowed whole.

Even as we stay shackled by Chinese rule, or remain in exile far and away from Tibet, this is something every Tibetan can do.

A Tibetan friend in Washington told me that every Tibetan New Year Tibetans around her celebrate following their tradition: plant barley shoots, make barley liquor, deep-fry *khapsay* (a kind of cookies) and *samkham papleg* (a dough kneaded with yak butter), and prepare offerings for the shrine, such as *droso chemar* (a mixture of barley flour, sugar and butter) and *luggo* (a sheep's head made of colored butter). When she was still living at home in Lhasa, all these were her elders' responsibilities; now she and other younger Tibetans have mastered the tasks.

During the Tibetan New Year, they have multi-family gatherings, tasting delicacies from Ü-Tsang, Amdo, and Kham Tibetan regions, belting out local tunes and chatting in local dialects. That is how they spend the New Year—*Losar*—à la Tibetan.

* * *

Contemporary Artists Sound Off

Is there contemporary art in Tibet?

Several years ago at an exhibition in Beijing's 789 Art Zone, even "the godfather of contemporary Chinese art," famed art critic Li Xianting, was awed by the works of seven Tibetan artists.

"I always thought Tibet had no contemporary art," Li said. "As soon as I saw this exhibition, the first thing that struck me was: Yes, Tibetans have their own contemporary art!"

Except for one who is British Tibetan, all the other artists hailed from a Lhasa-based group called Gedun Choephel Artists Guild. Although they had a hard time adapting to the heat in the mainland, they cherished their maiden opportunity to showcase their art in Beijing. Calling their exhibition "Inside Out,"[2] they underscore their desire to use art to document and expose the conditions of modern-day Tibet and speak for Tibetans. That is because as twenty-first-century Tibetans they find themselves in a superbly turbulent age complicated by the unprecedentedly entwined forces of globalization and sinicization, shattering the long lost tranquil isolation of the snow country on the plateau.

For the longest time, Tibetan art was known mostly for its *thangka* scrolls, murals in monasteries, and Buddha sculptures, etc. These are world-renowned representations of the dazzling chapters in the history of traditional Tibetan art. In the past few decades, the Tibetan art scene has been dominated by non-natives with their ideologically driven propaganda art, or saccharine, gilded depictions of Tibet as Shangri-la. It is a shame these misinterpretations have unduly impacted a generation of homegrown artists, who sought to free themselves from the stranglehold of tradition but felt that they had no voice.

So, once these artists set out to live by their principle to sound off, they, at long last, gave birth to contemporary Tibetan art—not just in Lhasa, but also in Beijing and New York. From then on they have found their unique voice. These young artists are buoyed by the great Tibetan intellectual humanist Gedun Choephel's spirit of resistance, and they know better: Breaking with tradition does not contemporary art make. Just as Li gave them this morsel of food for thought: "Contemporary art is not merely about the form, but more importantly it is about the concept. On the one hand, ancient Tibet may seem distant from our times; on the other, in Tibetan tradition there is no lack of contemporary concepts. For example, the sand mandala in Tibetan Buddhism is modern in form, concept and execution, far more so than most avant-garde art."

---

2.   This is the exhibition's English name. The Chinese name is *Fa Sheng Fa Sheng* 發生發聲, which translates into "come off, sound off."

A piece of Tibetan artist Gonkar Gyatso's performance art, called "My Identity Nos. 1–4," is a quadraptich of digital portraits of him as an artist in four different eras, thus illustrating the historical trajectory of an entire generation of Tibetans. The portraits show Gyatso working on canvases depicting, respectively, an abstract sand mandala, Buddha, Mao Zedong and the Dalai Lama. At the Beijing exhibition, the Dalai Lama frame was forbidden, leaving a blank in the installation. To me, the blank exactly extended his performance art—and exposed the condition of contemporary Tibet ever more vividly.

* * *

Resistance to Sell Out

In China, most Hans associate ethnic minorities only with song and dance. Indeed, the regime regards them as props, and parades them in colorful costumes in order to keep up appearances of harmony. At restaurants everywhere, minorities are human spices. They perform for diners and pose with tourists. . . .

Yet, a new generation of Tibetans is seeking to transform this stereotype. In Lhasa, there is a rock 'n' roll band called Vajara (Tianchu in Chinese), after a scepter-shaped ceremonial instrument used to cast off evil spirits. The band is disgusted with Tibetan pop, which is all about blue skies, white clouds, Tashi delek, and Shambhala within reach. The fact is, because there is nothing else to sing, even Tibetan prisoners are humming songs like "Let's Gather in Glee" and "Hope the Good Times Still Roll."

Vajara's members reject all aestheticism, romanticism and narcissism. They refuse to paint Tibet as Shangri-la. On stage, the band bellows to the audience: Come if you like to see our grasslands / They are all deserts now.

Their songs are critical of the apathy that has plagued fellow Tibetans. The lyrics go:

You parrot, you ape
You bob in the waves,
Did you give your brain away?
Don't you see many are in need?
Don't you see the world needs you to act?

Vajara's other lyrics deride people's desires:

Blinded by money, money, money
Grace you can't see
Love you no longer need . . .

——

Beautiful Rinzin Wangmo
I've fallen hard for you!
But you're all gems and jewels.
What am I to do?

The band also champions animal rights. Here is a song from the antelope's eye view:

Under the blue skies,
Lovely creatures thrive.
But here come humans the beasts.
They kill, they maim,
Their greed makes our world bleed.

The band members say they do not expect to be able to change the world, but they take comfort in knowing their fans now object to their parents donning fur. The bandmates are bonded by Buddhism, and the belief in benevolence preached by their faith. If their songs make their listeners more benevolent, the band members say they will be pleased.

To me, the arrival of Vajara means more than that: It signals the dawning of Tibetan people's self-consciousness. It is a refusal to be props and an insistence on independent thought, criticism and soul searching. Only a self-aware people is a dynamic people.

* * *

What Remains of Tibet?

Canadian-Tibetan Kalsang Dolma secreted into Tibet a short film on the Dalai Lama, and showed it to any Tibetan who crossed her path. Two documentary filmmakers accompanying her captured the audience's reactions. Most of the Tibetans shed tears at the sight of their spiritual leader. That the Dalai Lama remains banished from his homeland saddens many a Tibetan.

Called "What Remains of Us?" the film hits on a crucial issue: If the Dalai Lama is no more, then Tibetans will be left nothing. This points to his significance in Tibetans' eyes, which is at once true and truly worrisome.

Opinion polls in the West show the Dalai Lama surpasses the Pope in authority and prestige. Whenever Tibetans take pride in these polling results, do they ever wonder what other Tibetans have left their mark on the world? Since he cannot live forever, would this prediction not come true: Once the Dalai Lama is gone, Tibetans will be left with nothing?

Long ago, Tibetan artist Loten Namling has given this question some thought. In a comic strip, he depicts the Dalai Lama strenuously pulling a cart on a muddy path, and all Tibetans do is kneel inside the cart or along his way in prayer. Cartoon admittedly is an art of exaggeration, though very few Tibetans I have met within Chinese borders recognize their responsibility for Tibet's future. Most pin their hopes on him thousands of miles away.

Some say, perhaps Tibetan Buddhism puts much emphasis on karma, thus inculcating in Tibetans a lack of motivation and a belief in non-action. However, the future of a people is determined by their collective action. No matter how great a leader is, without followers he will remain an idol in a fantasy world, powerless to shape the destiny of his people.

Here is hoping beyond the halo of the Dalai Lama, there emerge more Tibetan leaders who shoulder the historical duties of their people and Tibetan talents in all arenas who take the world by storm. More importantly, only when Tibetans can harness the prowess of their fervent prayers to turn the wheel of history will they own Tibet's future. Only then can the Dalai Lama rest assured that even without him Tibet will not be lost, and his life's work will be carried on.

Epilogue

—by Woeser

In March 2013, China's legislature was set to meet in Beijing. Every time before a session, the CCP would guard against all potential sources of instability in its eye. Dissidents—including my husband and I—are either disappeared or put under house arrest.

In this very month, I received the International Women of Courage Award from the US State Department. This honor has plunged me into a cauldron of emotions.

I am a Tibetan born in Lhasa into a region long rocked by the CCP regime. From a tender age, I was taught in Chinese in an ideologically-driven education system. Never did I have a Tibetan class. And in university I majored in Chinese.

As a writer, I have found my conviction to write coming into focus gradually: To write is to experience; to write is to pray; to write is to bear witness. Experience, prayer and bearing witness all intertwine. And to bear witness is to give voice.

During their philosophical debate in search of meaning, Tibetan monks would clap in a steady, forceful crack. Their emphatic, rhythmic clapping signifies the golden truth of the Buddha's way.[1]

---

1. "The coming together of the two hands symbolizes the union of the two aspects of the path, wisdom and method, i.e. compassionate actions, . . . bringing (debaters) a clarity and a decisiveness that can help mobilize the intellectual capacities of the debaters and capture the attention of the audience." Georges B. Dreyfus, *The Sound of Two Hands Clapping: The Education of a Tibetan Monk* (Berkeley: University of California Press, 2003), 217.

As for me, by giving voice from the depths of my heart, I shower my sincerity upon a land that has nourished me and sing praises of my people's spirit. More often than not, however, the events of the day have impelled me to protest against my people's suffering as inflicted by the oppressors and restore historical memories so as to fend off state-sanctioned amnesia.

First, I penned poetry, using my verses to trace the veins of my roots. This was spiritual homecoming per my faith. Later, I launched into prose and fiction to depict Tibetan life. This has since opened my eyes to the misery and glory of the Tibetan people, as well as a myriad of real-life problems away from which I cannot turn my gaze. With an eye toward both history and reality, I set down to chronicle the happenings on my beloved Tibetan plateau.

But in March 2008, everything changed. The widespread unrest in the Tibetan regions was met with bloody suppression. The Chinese government stemmed the flow of news, turning up the decibels of its almighty propaganda machine and drowning out the voices of Tibet.

In order to bear witness as a writer, I began to give voice through as many channels as possible—books, blogs, radio programs, Twitter, Facebook, and press interviews. All these coalesced into "one-woman media."

My experience as one-woman media over the past few years has informed me how, for the powerless, the pen can be wielded as a weapon—a weapon honed by the Tibetan faith, tradition and culture. In face of the devastation Tibet has endured and the aspirations of Tibetans who have gone up in flames, I shall redouble my strength to resist oppression; I simply will not concede, or compromise.

Therefore, I wrote this to the State Department in response to my award: In Tibet today, countless of those who dared to give voice have been muffled by the regime's dark veil, and I myself am waiting for the axe to fall.

At this juncture, giving voice no doubt commands courage, but above all I hope voices are getting heard by those who listen, getting the attention from those who care, and getting help from those who seek to help. I hope citizens of conscience all over the world can join hands in redressing all injustices, delivering everyone from suffering, and restoring all rights to equality, liberty, and dignity. This is especially important, because even in the chilly long night of struggles we, too, take comfort in the warmth of your helping hands.

From the bottom of my heart, not only am I thankful for the International Women of Courage Award, I would also very much like to take it as a sign of concern for the blazing Tibetan plateau.

In truth, at this juncture, what I really want to say is: "I shall dedicate this award to all the Tibetans who have perished in self-immolation."

Source List

Barkor at Nightfall 對比深夜的 "太陽島" 和帕廓 (2006) by Wang Lixiong 王力雄. In Tsering Woeser and Wang Lixiong, *Voices from Tibet* 聽說西藏. Taipei: Locus Publishing, 2009.

Beijing Olympics: Divided World, Divided Dream 一場不但政治化，而且種族化的奧運會 (2008) by Tsering Woeser 唯色. In Woeser and Wang, *Voices from Tibet.*

Betting on Tibetan Land 西藏山河做賭場 (2006) by Wang Lixiong. In Woeser and Wang, *Voices from Tibet.*

Cassock vs. Police Uniform 當僧侶成為對手 (2008) by Wang Lixiong. In Woeser and Wang, *Voices from Tibet.*

Contemporary Artists Sound Off 發生和發聲中的西藏新藝術 (2007) by Tsering Woeser. In Woeser and Wang, *Voices from Tibet.*

Disappearing Lhasa 逐漸消失的拉薩 (2008) by Tsering Woeser. In Woeser and Wang, *Voices from Tibet.*

Every Inch of Land Is Sacred 仁青桑珠和他的鄉親們 (2011) by Wang Lixiong, http://wlx.sowiki.net/?action=show&id=388, accessed May 16, 2013.

Epilogue 我要把這個獎，獻給自焚的族人們！ (2013) by Tsering Woeser, http://www.rfa.org/mandarin/pinglun/weise/ws-03102013112314.html, accessed May 16, 2013.

Fall of Lhasa, The 拉薩？拉薩！ (2011) by Tsering Woeser, http://www.rfa.org/mandarin/pinglun/weise/weiser-10172011090613.html, accessed May 16, 2013.

Framing Monks as Terrorists 給藏人製造 "恐怖分子" 的證據 (2008) by Tsering Woeser. In Woeser and Wang, *Voices from Tibet.*

Freedom for Chinese, Autonomy for Tibetans 劉曉波先生說 "漢人無自由，藏人無自治" (2010) by Tsering Woeser, http://www.rfa.org/mandarin/pinglun/weise/ws-10152010132857.html, accessed May 16, 2013.

From Self-Immolation to Self-Rule 除了自焚，還能做什麼？ (2012) by Wang Lixiong, http://woeser.middle-way.net/2012/01/blog-post_14.html, accessed May 16, 2013.

Helicopters over Stupas 宗教與直升飛機 (2006) by Wang Lixiong. In Woeser and Wang, *Voices from Tibet*.

Herders Are Strangers on Their Land 重回半世紀前的勞改地 (2007) by Wang Lixiong. In Woeser and Wang, *Voices from Tibet*.

Highway Robbery in Holy Places 一個漢人的西藏挨宰記 (2007) by Wang Lixiong, and 在下密院欺騙遊客的是誰？(2007) by Tsering Woeser. In Woeser and Wang, *Voices from Tibet*.

How Fur Becomes Tibetan Fashion 獸皮"時尚"是如何產生的 (2006) by Wang Lixiong. In Woeser and Wang, *Voices from Tibet*.

Let Go of the Dalai Lama 讓達賴喇嘛不再是核心 (2011) by Wang Lixiong, http://wlx.sowiki.net/?action=show&id=413, accessed May 16, 2013.

Merchants of Fake Culture 黑心商人是如何打西藏牌的 (2007) by Tsering Woeser. In Woeser and Wang, *Voices from Tibet*.

Must Children Trade Roots for Books? 教育不應是文明的取代 (2005) by Wang Lixiong. In Woeser and Wang, *Voices from Tibet*.

Next Big One, The 西藏的下一次暴動 (2008) by Wang Lixiong. In Woeser and Wang, *Voices from Tibet*.

"Nineteenth Army", The 妓女和聖戰 (2005) by Wang Lixiong, and 西藏的愛滋病 (2007) by Tsering Woeser. In Woeser and Wang, *Voices from Tibet*.

Official Ban a Helpful Reminder 從一個個禁令中了解傳統和歷史 (2007) by Tsering Woeser. In Woeser and Wang, *Voices from Tibet*.

Only State-Sanctioned Tour Guides Need Apply 為什麼要從內地往西藏派導遊？(2006) by Wang Lixiong. In Woeser and Wang, *Voices from Tibet*.

Pernicious Fungus Economy, The 蟲草之害 (2007) by Wang Lixiong. In Woeser and Wang, *Voices from Tibet*.

Public Square or Propaganda? 文化帝國主義的廣場 (2005) by Wang Lixiong. In Woeser and Wang, *Voices from Tibet*.

Qinghai-Tibetan Railway Conscripted, The 青藏鐵路的新用途 (2008) by Tsering Woeser. In Woeser and Wang, *Voices from Tibet*.

Railroad to Perdition 沒有自治，青藏鐵路就不是"幸福路"(2007) by Tsering Woeser. In Woeser and Wang, *Voices from Tibet*.

Regret in a Half-Century 50年後你們會後悔的 (2011) by Wang Lixiong, http://wlx.sowiki.net/?action=show&id=431, accessed May 16, 2013.

Resistance to Sell Out "天杵"拒絕伴唱 (2006) by Wang Lixiong. In Woeser and Wang, *Voices from Tibet*.

Riding the Train to Lhasa (2012) 坐上了火車去拉薩…… (2012) by Tsering Woeser, http://www.rfa.org/mandarin/pinglun/weise/woser-10112012160236.html, accessed May 16, 2013.

Ringing in the Tibetan New Year 過藏曆新年：這是一種民族身分的象徵 (2008) by Tsering Woeser. In Woeser and Wang, *Voices from Tibet*.

Scrapping Tibetan Lessons for Stability 為了"維穩"取消藏語教學 (2012) by Tsering Woeser, http://www.rfa.org/mandarin/pinglun/weise/weise-03282012160055.html, accessed May 16, 2013.

Siphoning off Tibetan Water 誰來"模擬仿真"藏人的命運 (2007) by Wang Lixiong. In Woeser and Wang, *Voices from Tibet*.

Stampede in Jokhang 人滿為患的大昭寺 (2007) by Tsering Woeser. In Woeser and Wang, *Voices from Tibet*.

Tibetan Women Marry Han Chinese as a Way Out 走出大山的藏人少婦 (2006) by Wang Lixiong. In Woeser and Wang, *Voices from Tibet*.

Tibetans Are Ruined by Hope 藏人的夢想太多了 (2006) by Tsering Woeser. In Woeser and Wang, *Voices from Tibet*.

Where Are Tibetans in the Chinese Dream? "中國夢"裡有没有藏人的夢？(2013) by Tsering Woeser, http://www.rfa.org/mandarin/pinglun/weise/ws-03042013102653.html, accessed May 16, 2013.

What Remains of Tibet? 藏人還剩下什麼？(2007) by Wang Lixiong. In Woeser and Wang, *Voices from Tibet*.

Why Tibetans Flee to India? 藏人為何捨命逃印度？(2007) by Tsering Woeser. In Woeser and Wang, *Voices from Tibet*.

Winners and Losers under Tibet's Capitalism 西藏市場誰輸贏 (2005) by Wang Lixiong. In Woeser and Wang, *Voices from Tibet*.

World's Youngest Political Prisoner, The 全球最年幼的政治犯還是藏人 (2006) by Tsering Woeser. In Woeser and Wang, *Voices from Tibet*.

Ye All Celebrate Chinese Festivals 大一統的"中國表情" (2008) by Tsering Woeser. In Woeser and Wang, *Voices from Tibet*.

Bibliography

Barnett, Robert. *Lhasa: Streets with Memories*. New York: Columbia University Press, 2006.

Dreyfus, Georges B. *The Sound of Two Hands Clapping: The Education of a Tibetan Monk*. Berkeley: University of California Press, 2003.

Goldstein, Melvyn C., Dawei Sherap, and William R. Siebenschuh. *A Tibetan Revolutionary: The Political Life and Times of Bapa Phüntso Wangye*. Berkeley: University of California Press, 2006.

Hodous, Lewis and William E. Soothill. *A Dictionary of Chinese Buddhist Terms (with Sanskrit and English equivalents and a Sanskrit-Pali index)*. London: Kegan Paul, Trench, Trubner, 1937.

Larsen, Knud. *The Lhasa Atlas: Traditional Tibetan Architecture and Townscape*. Chicago: Serindia, 2001.

Liu, Xiaobo, et al. *No Enemies, No Hatred: Selected Essays and Poems*. Cambridge, MA: Harvard University Press, 2012.

van Schaik, Sam. *Tibet: A History*. New Haven: Yale University Press, 2011.